SHAKESPEARE
IN CHARGE

SHAKESPEARE IN CHARGE

The Bard's Guide to Leading and Succeeding on the Business Stage

NORMAN AUGUSTINE

and

KENNETH ADELMAN

tmb
talk miramax books
HYPERION

Library of Congress Cataloging-in-Publication Data

Augustine, Norman M.
    Shakespeare in charge : the bard's guide to leading and succeeding on the business stage / by Norman Augustine.—1st ed.
        p.   cm.
    1. Leadership.   2. Success in business.   3. Shakespeare, William. 1564–1616—Views on leadership.   4. Shakespeare, William. 1564–1616—Views on success in business.   I. Title.
    HD57.7.A848   1999
    658—dc21   99-42888
                                                                              CIP

ISBN 0-7868-6601-2

FIRST EDITION

10 9 8 7 6 5 4 3 2 1

To
Isabella
A star danced,
And under that star was she born.*

Greg
He had a daily beauty in his life,
But, O! the time of life is short.

Lawson
His very life was a jig.

and

William Shakespeare
omnium curiositatum explorator
the explorer of everything interesting

Born on Shakespeares's birthday, April 23, in 1998.

Contents

Credits

"They laugh that win," said Othello, who did neither. We're doing both since creating *Shakespeare in Charge* has been a series of wins for us.

The skilled Cordelia of the book world, Susan Mercandetti, matched us, just in the nick of time, with Jonathan Burnham, the editor-in-chief of Talk Miramax Books. We first launched this project even before *Shakespeare in Love* became a box office hit and won seven Oscars, including Best Picture of 1999.

Carried by the torrent of Bardmania, we knew the game was afoot. The major challenge of double-timing this book's creation enlivened us, much as Hotspur exclaimed in *Henry IV, Part I:* "O, the blood more stirs to rouse a lion than to start a hare!"

Jonathan Burnham, not only a fine person who, like Shakespeare, has British blood in his veins, "imagination bodies forth the forms of things unknown" and "turns them to shapes and gives to airy nothing a local habitation," as Theseus says in *A Midsummer Night's Dream*. This book is just one of Jonathan's many creative habitations.

We won with stylist Susan Suffes. Elaine Pofeldt did a superb job of research. She is "a scholar, and a ripe and good one, exceeding wise [and] fair-spoken," as Griffith says in *Henry VIII*. Arla Dittrick and Jean Ross did heroic work deciphering Norm's hieroglyphics.

Margaret Wolf did an exceptional job in copyediting this book, while Melanie Ross and Dennis Huston made sure the material stayed faithful to the Bard.

Gail Ross is our gifted literary agent and a particularly fine one. "Good counselors lack no clients," Pompey says in *Measure for Measure*.

We felt sheer joy and amazement working so closely with William Shakespeare, despite the four centuries separating us. Shakespeare's insights into human nature and his verbal creativity make him the world's most *under*rated genius.

And we rejoice as winners, big time, in the great mergers of our lives. Our marriages with Meg and Carol show the wisdom of Queen Isabel in *Henry V*: "God, the best maker of all marriages, combine your hearts in one, your realms in one!"

PROLOGUE

"To know the force of human genius, we should read Shakespeare," wrote essayist William Hazlitt. It's the genius revealed in the Bard's profound insights into human nature that has made him so extraordinarily successful for four hundred years.

Today, in our world barraged by entertainment options as never before, Shakespeare remains an undisputed star of stage and screen. His plays are staged more than other playwright's in the world's major cities and—in North America alone—form the basis for more than 140 Shakespearean summer festivals and theaters. Upward of 300 movies have been made of his plays, at least five in 1999 alone.

And Shakespeare is taught in more than 90 percent of American high schools and in all colleges. "Shakespeare is the best mind-altering substance I know," said English professor Helen Whall of the College of Holy Cross.

Many business executives think they lack the time for Shakespeare, or the training to understand his archaic language. (Shakespeare, typically, predicted such a response: "'Tis ten to one," the spokesman wagers in the Epilogue to *Henry VIII,* that "this play can never please all that are here." Some in the audience may even have "come to take their ease and sleep an act or two.")

But a growing number of executives find that time spent with the Bard is a sound investment, and unpredictably enjoyable. The Bard boom has hit the boardroom. For business leaders find that Shakespeare's plays offer deft and gripping explorations of the world of power which remain as relevant today as they were in the sixteenth century. The lessons they teach are remarkably useful in today's tough corporate universe.

At first blush, it might seem that Shakespeare and modern management don't mesh. Shakespeare conjures up images of crazy princes, ugly witches, fallen kings, and sulking guys in tights holding skulls of worthy corpses. The word *management* conjures up images of crazy prices, ugly deals, fallen CEOs, and sulking guys in gray suits holding stacks of worthless options.

But the two *do* mesh. For business involves people, and people—fundamentally—don't change. The essence of business is thus remarkably constant.

While the accoutrements of corporate life are now dramatically high tech—dominated by e-mail, cell phones, the Web, and PCs—the basics still hinge on human nature. Corporate affairs remain dependent largely on the strengths or failings of the men and women who make up a company or organization. The darker side of human nature—greed, overreaching ambition, ravaging jealousy, dishonesty—is as likely to undermine or even destroy a business now as it was before the days of the Internet and pagers. And, as we shall see, it is this darker side that Shakespeare understands so well.

Not all business recapitulates Shakespearean tragedy, of course. But neither do they habitually achieve the happy ending of the Bard's comedy. Success is difficult to achieve at any level. Many modern executives face a series of obstacles along their path that require intense understanding and careful handling. As Rosalind puts it in *As You Like It*, "How full of briers is this working day world." A study of Shakespeare can teach us, in our "working day world," how best to handle those "briers." For he offers the most penetrating insights into what makes people and organizations tick at every level.

Shakespeare is fascinated by the depths and complications of human relationships: boss to subordinate, colleague to colleague, lawyer to client, customer to salesperson, parent to child, and friend to friend. And he probes the range of human emotions—ambition, hurt, pride, grief, and love—as well as portraying the motivation behind our acts, wise or foolish, generous or malicious.

Across the Shakespearean stage strolls every type of human leader, manager, advisor, consultant, communicator, and customer. Each of these characters can deepen our awareness of the real people we work with and meet every day. Being able to recognize these types helps us to understand them, and means we're able to deal with them more effectively.

Take Nestor, an obscure character in a reasonably obscure play, *Troilus and Cressida*. Nestor, we're told by everyone, including himself—repeatedly!—is old, respected, and wise. His advice is given in the interminable war council for the interminable Trojan War, which is into its seventh year when the play *opens*.

Nestor presents his advice, and colleagues show the appropriate respect. It is not until we've heard him several times that it dawns on us that he expounds laboriously what speakers before him say crisply. To another's nugget of thought, Nestor adds neither depth nor breadth. When everything's already been said, he keeps on saying it.

Once we've perceived that Nestor contributes nothing but reiterates everything, we heighten our ability to recognize the real Nestors who prattle on in boardrooms, executive suites, conferences, and courtrooms all over America. Listening to Nestors can be maddening, but knowing it's a Nestor we're listening to can help us to be more wary.

Every business, too, has its Kent, the loyal retainer in *King Lear*. Kents will never run an organization or command real power, but they contribute their best when working closely with the CEO (or King), counseling, correcting, knowing the King better than he knows himself, and staying faithful. Lear, the old foolish king, impulsively banishes his favorite daughter Cordelia when she is unwilling to proclaim excessive love for him. Lear then banishes Kent, too, when he violently objects.

But types like Kent are not easy to fire. Shakespeare's Kent disguises himself and returns to serve Lear through the storm on the heath and the thousand afflictions he endures. While recognizing Lear's flaws, Kent still regards him as "every inch a king" and epitomizes the loyalist, even after Lear's death. A Kent is worth keeping on the payroll.

His counterpart, the Fool, is less conventional than Kent, but just as valuable. Every organization has its "court jesters" who joke and fool around but often articulate—through their jokes—an unpalatable truth, and are able to speak to the boss in a way that no one else will dare. Lear laughs at the Fool but recognizes that his clowning conceals shrewd advice. It is the Fool who advises Lear—and us, incidentally—to "have more than thou showest, speak less than thou knowest, lend less than thou owest."

Executives should watch out for characters like Cassius in *Julius Caesar:* highly competent but destructively resentful. As we will see in our closer examination in Act III, Cassius has a sharp mind and sound judgment, but he bridles under supervision, which limits his effectiveness on a team where clear reporting structures and trust are crucial.

Also on the "executive beware" list is the absentee leader. This is the CEO or boss who is constantly traveling, living far from headquarters, or so engaged in extracurricular activity that he loses any sense of priorities. He ignores the admonition of Lepidus in *Antony and Cleopatra:* "Small to greater matters must give way."

He speaks before the arrival of Antony, who was a skillful soldier, loyal friend, steadfast man of action and communicator par excellence in *Julius Caesar.* Antony has been indulging in a life of pleasure in Egypt, where

Cleopatra's seductive powers hold him. He is sufficiently self-aware to admit how far he has strayed: "These strong Egyptian fetters I must break, or lose myself in dotage," but in fact he doesn't manage to break away. Finally a military defeat caused by Cleopatra leads to Antony's personal humiliation and the ruin of his reputation, and then a botched suicide. Luckily, most corporate absenteeism does not result in such drastic dénouements.

Shakespeare's plays are full of characters that can be studied for useful corporate analogies, but *Shakespeare in Charge* focuses on five plays in particular, and five characters.

Act I explores overall leadership through the glorious feats of Henry V. New on the throne and forced to prove himself, he uses time-tested leadership techniques to succeed most royally. Watching Henry's skill in deploying these techniques gives top executives some useful lessons in the art of leadership.

Act II queues off the cyberoptic speed of change in today's business. A popular comedy, *The Taming of the Shrew* shows how Petruchio, its pivotal character, both reacts to and implements change in people and institutions.

Act III is filled with nuts-and-bolts advice from *Julius Caesar* on getting the job done in business—goalsetting, recruitment, team-building and operations, corporate communications, and more.

Act IV delves into the art and danger of risk-taking found in abundance in the only Shakespearean play named after a businessman, *The Merchant of Venice*, and starring its most adept executive, Portia. She and others must "give and hazard all"—risky business indeed.

And Act V shows what happens when risks go bad or when avoiding risks makes for bad business—or when bad things just happen. Crisis management consumes Claudius in Shakespeare's most intriguing and popular play, *Hamlet*.

Throughout we offer Shakespeare's plots and words in a user-friendly way, tailored to the busy corporate executive. Aside from our readings and personal interpretations of key Shakespearean scenes, we present crisp business lessons drawn from the play at hand. These are supported by other Shakespearean examples, as well as by stories from the contemporary business stage.

We are not academics, and this is not intended to be an objective critical assessment of Shakespeare. The aim is to open up Shakespeare's wisdom for the business reader and pair it with our own experience as practical men who have worked in the corporate and political worlds at a high level.

When we started writing this book in 1997, we felt like pioneers. Since then, Columbia University's School of Business began offering its MBA students a business course called "In Search of the Perfect Prince," centered on case studies from Shakespeare. And in June of 1999 Britain's Cranfield University School of Business launched a cooperative venture with the Globe Theatre, under Richard (son of Sir Laurence) Olivier, in which executives can spend a weekend at the Globe learning about global business from Shakespeare's plays.

It seems significant that others are setting out to

teach business courses based on Shakespeare at a time when business itself is changing at a swifter pace than ever before. It perhaps confirms that the wisdom of one of the world's greatest minds can be made useful to a smart executive in a risky world.

"Speak on, but be not over-tedious," says Burgundy in *Henry VI, Part I*. We have spoken on long enough for a Prologue. Knowing our intentions, executives can now proceed into the Acts. "All things are ready, if our minds be so!" as Henry V declares at the outset of his adventure.

ACT I

ON LEADERSHIP

"What Impossible Matter Will

He Make Easy Next?"

[DRAMATIS EXECUTIVUS SUMMARIUS]

In any organization—whether the English army of the fifteenth century or the global corporation of the twenty-first—strong and wise leadership makes all the difference.

Superb leadership, of the type King Henry V displays, can compensate for shocking shortcomings elsewhere. Likewise, weak leadership, of the type many other Shakespearean kings exhibit, can just as readily undermine extensive strengths.

The appointment of the right leader can rescue the most perilous predicament. Projects involving thousands of people have been turned around by the single act of installing the most suitable person at the top. It's not so much that this person individually accomplishes so much work; Shakespeare doesn't report that King Henry personally slew hordes of French soldiers on the fields of Agincourt. Rather, it's that a charismatic and competent leader creates an environment that allows, indeed propels or inspires, so many others to accomplish so much.

This is the stuff of tales vividly told by Shakespeare and by contemporary corporate success stories alike. But we dare any to match the Bard's narrative of true grit, grand strategizing, sheer competence, dogged perseverance, and creativity shown by King Henry V.

Shakespeare's breathtaking account—amplified by a few historical facts—is one worth not only recounting but scrutinizing for a very sound reason. Henry presents clear lessons for today's corporate executive about the central question: "How can I, as an executive, excel as a leader?"

PROLOGUE

Oddly enough, Henry V is one of the Bard's few kings who is good and does well. Other Shakespearean kings, like Richard III, Claudius, and Macbeth, exude leadership—but their flawed natures vastly overshadow their competence.

Others among Shakespearean kings—Richard II in his one play, Henry IV in his two plays, and Henry VI in his three plays—don't really lead anyone to do much of anything.

Henry V's father, Henry IV, is the best of the lot

(primarily because they are such a sorry group), but he's a leader in campaigning, not in governing. When named Bolingbroke, he masterfully takes power, but later, he exercises it amateurishly. He's also a distinctly uninteresting man, even when accomplishing such a stellar management feat as winning a come-from-nowhere campaign to oust an incumbent divine-right ruler.

Plagued with afflictions, both personal and political, he becomes a sick, boring bureaucrat. His initial worry, consolidating his illegitimate reign, ends up as his sole concern. This is a syndrome not unknown to CEOs, some of whom focus less on what they can accomplish while in the job than on how to accomplish staying in the job.

In contrast, Richard II, the King he overthrew, is a "sweet lovely rose" as a man but an utter failure as a ruler. With incredible drama and poetry, Richard II yields up his power. He lacks everything in resistance but nothing in artistry. It's as if Richard, rather than *command* as real king, would much rather *play* the role of fallen king.

Another of Shakespeare's pathetic royals, Henry VI, is just weak. The poor fellow had never wanted to be king, and never should have been. Henry VI epitomizes the dangers of a family business passed along on the basis of birth rather than merit. Sometimes this works, but it does defy the odds. He also shows the woes that commonly befall children—especially sons—of great leaders.

Happily, in Henry V we have a man at the apex of both the power and leadership scales. Watching Henry up-close-and-personal shows us a leader working brilliantly with his executive staff and lowly subordinates alike, a grand strategist who focuses on detail, a man whose private doubts and fears remain concealed as his public persona exudes confidence, a motivational speaker who peps up his team right before they take the field, and a warrior-commander who inspires them and drives them on to victory.

SCENE I

[Curtain rises. Enter shiny-faced youth wearing a crown.]

Just twenty-seven years old and known dissolute, Prince Hal becomes King Henry V once his father finally expires. Taking his new role seriously, Henry renounces drinking and cavorting with his pal Falstaff to begin ruling a kingdom that is, to be generous, rather wobbly.

The family business has not been going well. Henry's father, Henry IV, had a woeful reign notable for rebellion of all sizes, shapes, and types. His advice to his son was succinct: Go for an acquisition, even if it entails a hostile takeover. In fifteenth-century England, that meant finding someplace to attack—it didn't much matter where—in order to "busy giddy minds" at home "with foreign quarrels."

Like any new and especially young executive, Henry longs to make his mark. War offers a great opportunity to do so—but only if he wins.

As it happens, one such opportunity arises right away. From his new throne, the King seeks advice from his top nobles and clergy, most of whom still doubt his ability to rule. Henry thereby gives his first glimmer of leadership; he senses the need for inclusion. The more people consulted on a major decision, he realizes, the more the staff feels a part of that decision and gains a stake in its outcome. The problem, however, is that his consultants are knee-deep in conflicts of interest, a fact no CEO should ever overlook.

So Henry, gathering the powerful group, listens carefully to their ponderous religious and legal justifications for his claim to rule France. The clergy back the move to grab far-off French land for turf reasons. They hope to preclude the King from joining those who seek to appropriate their nearby church properties. The men of the cloth essentially swap their support for Henry's war in exchange for his support for their land holdings. Such unholy dealings are not foreign to modern corporate politics.

The nobles also itch to fight, as many seem eager to plunder. Their perspective is expressed by the nonnoble, ignoble Pistol: "Let us to France, like horse leeches, my boys. To suck, to suck, the very blood to suck!"

Once everyone is thus consulted and signs on to his ambitious quest, Henry shows decisiveness, another essential leadership trait. He knows that a crisp and timely executive decision is almost invariably preferable to a more ideal decision later.

Henry thus fearlessly mobilizes his army to advance onto French lands. But even before he's gained any on-the-throne training, Henry confronts two mega-crises.

First, a trio of his top lieutenants, boyhood friends all, conspire to capitalize on his flightiness and inexperience.

Unfortunately for them, they get their man wrong, for Henry's neither shortsighted nor naive. Indeed, throughout the play he shows brilliant insight into other peoples' character, a key executive attribute.

Having sensed treachery afoot and learned that the threesome have lined their doublets with French gold, he accuses them of treason. Trapped, they confess. Henry graciously hears their pleas—and then orders them executed on the spot.

The second crisis comes when Bardolph, Henry's former drinking buddy, is caught looting a French church, flouting the King's strict order to refrain from plundering. There's no royal pardon from Bardolph's ex-barmate. He, too, is executed. The parade must go on. (At this point it's rather ironic that, in this classic tale of intense combat, the most prominent killing thus far has been within the English army.)

By taking such bold action early on, Henry shows the need to carefully evaluate his key staff and eliminate the bad seeds. Finding them, he gives them the *ultimate* pink slip.

While usually avoiding such extreme measures, true leaders must make bold personnel decisions, understanding the risk of *not* doing so. That is, after all, one of the things that makes them leaders. "To be tender-minded does not become a sword," Edmund says in *King Lear*. Even in a large and complicated organization, just one of thousands of employees can plunge the entire organization into an abyss. That is precisely what happened to the esteemed Barings Bank in 1995. Knowingly overlooking malperformance sends a dreadful message to all diligent employees who know what is going on. At best they see vice or incompetence rewarded; at worst they feel encouraged to embark on hazardous, unproductive paths themselves.

As severe as it is, Henry's tough behavior serves another executive purpose. Every organization develops a certain style and manner, a distinct personality and pattern of behavior that are largely set at the top. "Princes are the glass, the school, the book wherein subjects' eyes do learn, do read, do look," Shakespeare wrote in his early poem "The Rape of Lucrece." Others in the organization receive signals, both consciously and subconsciously, whether from the king, "princes," CEO, or supervisors. They use them as models to conclude, "So that's the way things are done around here." Such signals establish patterns to guide individual behavior throughout the corporation.

Henry's foot soldiers see that he treats friends just as he would treat them. They, like staff in any firm, judge whether those at the top act fairly and, if they do, behave likewise to *their* underlings, work harder, and keep to the rules.

Meanwhile, during his traipsing through France, Henry meets resistance in the French town of Harfleur. He brutally threatens its governors: Know that "bloody soldier[s] with foul hand [would] defile the locks of your shrill-shrieking daughters," and see the town's old men "taken by the silver beards, and their most reverend heads dashed to the walls."

Henry's bold tactic, perhaps a bluff, succeeds nicely. Without any such atrocity, the French yield voluntarily.

Still, one French town giving way does not a celebrated leader make. Henry is lucky, because a leader cannot make a career out of threats and bluffs nor expect to draw an ace every time. Sooner or later, the odds catch up.

Once Henry and his army march far into enemy territory, they face overwhelming opposition. The King's strategic assessment has not matched his personnel acuity. When his army finally reaches the field of Agincourt, his exhausted troops realize that they've landed in trouble—big time.

French soldiers outnumber Henry's forces enormously, the English think by at least five to one. Moreover, the French are well rested and well fed; over a thousand French officers, astride fresh steeds, sport sparkling armor. Most important, the French soldiers know that they're fighting to defend their country, their wives, and their children.

In contrast, most of the English troops, wearing tattered clothes, have trudged across half of France—few had horses to ride—and are utterly exhausted. They resent being underfed, overfatigued, underequipped, and, especially, over there. Worse yet, the reason for invading France escapes them. They would prefer to escape France.

Nonetheless, Henry pushes them forward under appalling conditions, which displays persistence, another of his executive talents. Only individuals who persist ultimately achieve.

Still, it's no wonder that, on the very eve of battle, Henry's men are scared out of their wits. Many must doubt the King's staying power. They even question whether they're in the right business, and they come to feel that it's an exceptionally inopportune occasion to launch a hostile takeover. Wholesale slaughter seems imminent, with little question over who's to be slaughtered. And for what?

Therefore it's no surprise that, on the drizzly morning of October 25, 1415, the top staff gathers to wonder what's to become of them that day. "Where is the King?" one asks, worried whether he'll even show up to work that morning.

Unbeknownst to them, they are about to go from the depths of depression to the heights of joy, because Henry the King is about to become Henry the Leader.

SCENE II

[Enter a drained, drenched king, struggling on the sodden field of Agincourt]

Though the situation with his men remains precarious, Henry V firms up his plans. While trudging through France, he's enumerated the assets he can apply to the battle—longbows, stakes, swords, lances, barricades, daggers, battleaxes, and the like. All these things are necessary but not, in themselves, sufficient to win the battle. People, properly motivated and deployed, constitute his best asset. The same is true in business.

Practicing walk-around management rare among royals, Henry, in disguise, strolls among his troops on the eve of battle, "a little touch of Harry in the night," as Shakespeare tenderly calls it.

However, there's nothing tender in the message

Harry le Roy (as Henry calls himself) receives. The staff hasn't bought into his strategic plan. As many executives have learned to their dismay, goals dictated solely from the top seldom win the devotion of those who must implement them.

A more seasoned executive would have anticipated this and other key arguments from the disgruntled group, and would have prepared keener counterarguments. Henry's rejoinders to his troops aren't convincing, primarily because they're so abstract.

Nevertheless, by strolling among his men, the King makes an extraordinary effort to probe their inner thoughts and feelings. He listens to others' opinions and respects their fears.

Henry's men could care deeply about being part of a cause that rises above themselves, if they only knew of such a cause. Handled right, it could cloak them in fame and pride for the rest of their lives. People love to be part of a winning team, and success begets success. The opposite, of course, is true, too, which is why danger lurks in the shadows of any executive who permits an organization to suffer a series of losses. Under such circumstances, an executive must take drastic measures.

Building on what he hears and knows instinctively, Henry formulates a stirring message that will lift his troops from the role of ordinary foot soldiers to celebrated heroes with astonishing courage and skill.

Out of his ragtag lot, Henry molds a first-rate team, stirred by his stunning St. Crispin's Day speech delivered the next morning before the battle. Among the most glorious of English speeches, it is a masterpiece of motivational oratory, used as a model ever since by coaches (especially, like Henry, before away matches).

Before Henry begins, the nobles gather on the battlefield. The Earl of Warwick articulates what's on everyone's mind, namely that the French have as many as "full [sixty thousand] fighting men." The Earl of Exeter fearmongers further, exclaiming, "There's five to one. Besides, they all are fresh!" The Lord of Salisbury heaps on more doom, moaning, "God's arm strike with us! 'Tis a fearful odds."

Their frightened talk exemplifies Shakespeare's keen insight into group dynamics. When doubts arise, they grow exponentially unless stemmed and reversed hard and fast. This is as true in modern business as in medieval armies. No business should tolerate doomsayers within the ranks of its leaders—they can be a fatal corporate malignancy.

Henry, tapped into the mindsets and attitudes of his men, sizes up the situation as soon as he arrives on the scene. Then, significantly, Westmoreland tells the King he wishes that one-ten-thousandth of the men lounging around England that day were with them there.

At this, Henry begins to turn the mood around by addressing spot-on his men's concerns. He points out that, "No, my fair cousin. If we are marked to die, we are enough to do our country loss." Yet if they are to live, "the fewer men, the greater share of honour."

In a bit of bravado, Henry insists that anyone who "hath no stomach to this fight [let him] depart." Any man wishing to scram will even receive walk-away money, for

Henry doesn't want such a man in his army. "We would not die in that man's company."

Speaking with mounting force and in the interests of sound leadership, King Henry keeps reminding his troops that this is a sacred day, "the Feast of Crispin." The religious aspects of the feast reinforce Henry's constant evocation of God and prayer, thereby helping to unify the group into a holy crusade. And the feast celebrates two saints, brothers with the oddly similar names Crispian and Crispin, who were humble shoemakers celebrated for their service, just as Henry's lowly foot soldiers will be celebrated for theirs.

To Henry, the "Feast of Crispin" will be overshadowed by the feats of his men, who fight to bring victory. On the anniversary of this day forevermore, each veteran will feast his neighbors. "Then will he strip his sleeve and show his scars and say, 'These wounds I had on Crispin's Day.'"

Stirring them on, he tells them that all of England will recall, intoning, "Then shall our names [become] familiar in his mouth as household words." From then on and forever, "this story shall the good man teach his son" and St. Crispin's Day shall never pass "from this day to the ending of the world" without a celebration of their victory.

Henry thus projects the future pride that will stem from their coming victory. Characteristically he never questions the win, but simply presumes it. Like all adept executives, as key decision-maker he must exude complete confidence that this is the right—indeed, the only sensible—option. Whether on the battlefield of Agincourt, the financial hub of Wall Street, or the stores of Main Street, others won't follow a leader who blows an uncertain trumpet.

Henry continues to bind the group into a cohesive, highly motivated unit: "We few, we happy few, we band of brothers. For he today that sheds his blood with me shall be my brother."

Suddenly the Earl of Salisbury rides up to report. "The French are bravely in their battles set and will, with all expedience, charge on us." At this point Montjoy, the suave French envoy, gallops up to ask Henry to turn back and avoid scores of English deaths in certain defeat. Henry tells him to get lost. The Battle of Agincourt has begun.

Henry's St. Crispin's Day speech proves pivotal. It transforms his grumbling group of journeymen into a cohesive band of warriors. Successful corporate leaders inspire people to dig deep within themselves, which makes that critical difference between victory and defeat. Henry's words penetrate deeply since his men, like all humans everywhere, relish connecting with one another as part of a splendid mission. Working toward and winning a lofty goal will glorify each of them individually and all of them collectively.

Still, while Henry recognizes that people matter most, he doesn't rely on pep rallies alone, no matter how well they turn out, to deliver the victory. Amassing other assets, he brilliantly transforms military disadvantages into distinct advantages. By so doing, Henry demonstrates unrivaled competence. This is essential in political, military, and modern corporate operations. Henry plants his men in a strong defensive position to prepare for the coming French attack reported by Salisbury. Waiting for the French to strike tactically affords him a huge advantage.

This is a major decision, one that shows sound judgment and clear thinking based on the facts. The steady rain, which has depressed and exhausted the soldiers, becomes a key ally. It bogs down the enemy cavalry charging on the steady English troops. The French, who always care about looking good, are burdened by their elaborate shining armor, which weighs up to an oppressive seventy pounds per man. Their horses sink deep in the mud.

At the same time, relentless longbow attacks from Henry's archers thin out the waterlogged French forces. The Welsh forests—the Silicon Valley of that era—furnish flexible wood and, more impressively, imaginative brains to turn the local trees into potent longbows. Deploying those assets gives the English a high-tech—or, more aptly, a high-arch—advantage that the low-tech French can't match.

Henry also shows sharp judgment in another tactic. He has his men dig in defensively and pitch wooden spikes, which gouge any charging French horses or even infantry forces that manage to survive the archers' robust assault. Moreover, Henry positions his men and spikes to funnel the oncoming French forces into a relatively confined area.

Henry has obviously mastered the basic skills and knowledge of his field—in this case, the battlefield. As commander-in-chief, Henry would have to have known military strategy and tactics. (Some modern corporate boards presume that CEOs who succeed in one field can do so in another, only to learn that it takes Henryesque knowledge of the field to defeat the toughest competition.) Henry also realizes that no one action will suffice; he needs a grand strategic plan to win his grand battle.

His talents are crucial since, at Agincourt, the fighting is ferocious. Presumably Henry bravely wages hand-to-hand combat alongside his men, showing the type of courage displayed by virtually all great leaders at critical points in their careers. In times of crisis there is only one place for a leader to be, and that place is not safely back in the castle.

Still, success has thus far eluded Henry. While he's shown executive vision, persistence, judgment, competence, and courage, he is far from perfect. At a critical moment on the battlefield, King Henry panics and makes a terrible mistake that haunts him forevermore.

Scene III

[Enter young soldiers wearing blood-soaked clothes and ferociously swinging their swords]

In almost all human pursuits, whether business, combat, or athletics, at some critical point the outcome hinges in the balance, when the course of events can turn in either direction. That is the point at which leadership must be at its zenith.

Midbattle reports, based less on hard facts than mere rumor, speed from soldier to soldier. Shakespeare's portrayal of confusion and ignorance in a fast-breaking situation rings true. The lack of accurate and timely information is a normal affliction for any leader in such a predicament. Supposedly in charge, the leader remains largely in the dark.

Even sounds are misinterpreted. Deep into the battle, Henry hears something from afar and reckons the "new alarum" signifies "the French have reinforced their scattered men." Acting characteristically fast, he sends out an irrevocable order: "Then every soldier kill his prisoners." Such a command is clearly against the laws of war, which protect noncombatants. This was a horrid mistake. Some reports indicate that Henry's regular forces refused to follow this order and that he had to use special forces for the slaughtering. Shakespeare must have felt deep regret for his young hero over this barbarism, for the Bard ends the scene quickly and next has regular soldiers commenting on this "knavery."

Still, the main action is proceeding much as Henry planned. The English force the advancing French into an area vulnerable from three sides. The British soldiers clobber their enemy mightily as many of the French troops are simply too exhausted to defend themselves.

Nevertheless, confusion still reigns. Even the King wonders what's happening in the grand scheme of battle, surely appreciating how slight is the margin between total victory and utter defeat, grand success and dismal failure.

Finally Henry learns of the remarkable victory from

a most authoritative source. The French envoy Montjoy tells him simply, "The day is yours."

Henry is ecstatic, as well he should be. Fewer than thirty are lost on his side versus some ten thousand lost by the French!

Not surprisingly, historians credit the leadership of Henry V with turning the Battle of Agincourt into one of the most astonishing victories in history.*

Exeter closes the battlefield discussion of their victory with a comment as apt as it is short. He concludes, "'Tis wonderful."

ACTING LESSONS

"He was indeed the glass wherein the noble youth did dress themselves," Hotspur's young widow says of her departed warrior in *Henry IV, Part I*. Likewise, today's corporate executives can regard Henry V as the "glass" wherein they can dress their leadership. From his impressive talents, which brought England glorious victory, contemporary execs can take away eight critical lessons on leadership.

---

*The historical numbers are a bit more modest but still stunning. According to John Keegan in *The Face of Battle* (New York: Viking Press, 1976), which examines history's most dramatic military battles, the English were outnumbered at Agincourt by at least three to one and as much as thirty to one. During the battle, the English lost only a handful of men while the French buried about 6,000 (page 113).

LESSON ONE

"Stand like greyhounds in the slips,
straining upon the start."

—King Henry V

Executives must stand poised to take immediate advantage of opportunities as they arise.

From *Henry V*'s opening scenes to its close, Henry exhibits true grit and raw determination while seizing opportunities. Despite being new on the job, whether on the throne or on the battlefield, he never lets uncertainty, or circumstances, or obstacles deter him. Nor does he wait for all possible information on the topic to present itself and be duly evaluated before he acts.

Henry understands the importance of timing in achieving goals. As Brutus says in *Julius Caesar,* "There is a tide in the affairs of men which taken at the flood leads on to fortune; omitted, all the voyage of their life is bound in shallows and in miseries." While shrewd business leaders do as much careful research as possible before investing time or money into a new venture, they know that resources are limited and time has a value all its own. Like Henry, they learn about the situation, follow their instincts, and act determinedly.

Richard Branson, the charismatic British entrepreneur, mirrored the charismatic British king in not waiting for extensive market research before launching his venture. He made as snappy a decision to go into flight with Virgin Atlantic airline in 1984 as Henry made to charge into France.

When Branson phoned People's Express and kept

getting busy signals, he concluded that "they must be doing really well or they're really inefficient. If either was true, I figured there was room for competition." He promptly bought a single 747 and began flying customers. He felt akin to Mercutio in *Romeo and Juliet*: "In delay, we waste our lights in vain, like lamps by day."

To establish a competitive advantage, Branson offered long-distance passengers first-class seating at business-class prices in its Upper Class program. Widely recognized for excellence, Virgin Atlantic was named Best Transatlantic Airline by *Travel Weekly* each year from 1988 to 1999. Virgin's Upper Class service was voted Best Transatlantic Business Class by readers of *Condé Nast Traveler* in 1998.

Today, Virgin Atlantic services London from eight U.S. cities and flies to South Africa, Greece, the Caribbean, Japan, China, and Hong Kong out of London. The airline logged sales of $1.4 billion for fiscal 1998, up 7.7 percent from fiscal 1997. In April 1999, one of Branson's executives announced that they were considering taking the company public on both the London and U.S. stock markets.

When Todd Wagner told his friend Mark Cuban that listening to broadcasts of Indiana basketball games on the Internet would be really great, they took the ball and ran with it. Purchasing about $5,000 worth of computer equipment, they set up shop in Cuban's spare bedroom in the summer of 1995. Cuban, who had started a successful computer consulting business right out of Indiana University, taught himself to master the technology necessary to get their company on the air.

By September, the two buddies had boldly approached KLIF, a Dallas talk-radio station, with an offer to turn their idea into a moneymaking business. Walking into the station, they must have felt as Falstaff did in *Henry IV, Part I,* when he said, "Well, God give [us] the spirit of persuasion and [them] the ears of profiting, that what [we] speakest may move and what [they] hear may be believed."

KLIF agreed to let the guys tape its broadcasts, digitize the recordings, and post them on their Web site. That was the beginning of Broadcast.com.

Today, visitors who log onto the site can listen to their local radio stations or watch nationwide local television news. Wall Street has tuned in, too. The company has a capitalization of nearly $4.2 billion. As Exeter would have said, "'Tis wonderful."

LESSON TWO

"'Tis true that we are in danger; the greater
therefore should our courage be."

—King Henry V

Courage to stand up to a major challenge and willingness to plunge ahead are hallmarks of true corporate leadership. Showing true grit sets a standard that motivates employees like few others.

Approaching a deadly battle where his army is woefully outnumbered, Henry urges his men to face the enemy head-on. He doesn't just talk the talk, he walks the walk by leading his soldiers into the fray.

Executives endowed with such courage in the face of overwhelming odds resemble the valor of the flea described by Orleans, one of the French nobles in *Henry V*: "You may as well say that's a valiant flea that dares eat his breakfast on the lip of a lion." Partnering courage with more judgment than that flea has is as important for seizing a competitive edge today as it was for Henry in his day.

Jake Burton, designer of the snowboard, has peered down many a slippery slope. He believes his company, privately held Burton Snowboards, has an advantage over bigger competitors like Nike and Adidas because he himself is addicted to the risky sport of boarding. "Even when we do an ad that's designed to appeal to the mainstream," he says, "we do one that hardcore riders can respect."

The company, based in Burlington, Vermont, counts five hundred employees and brings in an estimated $150 million in annual gross sales. In 1998 his snowboards gained international recognition when they were used in the Olympics.

Despite his exceptional success, Burton doesn't want to take the company public. He has an unconventional way of running his organization, in large part because Burton is an unconventional person. Like the Prince of Arragon in *The Merchant of Venice*, he does not want to "jump with common spirits and rank me with the barbarous multitudes."

When the snow is right, Burton has been known to close the business early and let the entire staff spend the rest of the workday snowboarding. He says, "No one ever lost their job at this place for snowboarding too much."

Another reason for maintaining the courage of his conviction is his high standard of quality control. Specifically he wants to avoid the compromises that public companies often tolerate to keep short-term earnings high for impatient shareholders. "We need to make long-term decisions that can adversely affect short-term profits," he points out. "You notice we have not sold Burton in-line skates, underwear, or bran muffins. Stockholders would be tempted to try all that." His formula is working. Burton Snowboards controls an estimated 45 percent of the market.

LESSON THREE

"All things are ready if our minds be so."

—King Henry V

Beyond courage, corporate executives must display persistence over a long period and against staggering odds. While few events are as terror-filled as war on foreign soil with overwhelming opposition in troops and equipment, Henry persists. Whatever it takes, he's determined to win—and he does.

That determination summons the most possible from within himself and from his troops as they, too, persist. This truth Shakespeare dramatizes in comic form through Petruchio's efforts in *The Taming of the Shrew*. As we detail in the next Act, Petruchio identifies a goal (a rich wife), devises a business strategy, and pursues his prey (the shrew Katherine) with exceptional energy and imagination. His first tactic is honeyed compliments. Katherine spurns him, insults him, even strikes him. Petruchio sees that this approach is not working, but undeterred, he comes up with an entirely new plan, this one forceful and threatening (under the guise of concern for her well-being). When Katherine shows signs of compliance, he continues implementing this improved tactic until he overcomes her resistance and brings out the best in her. She is converted into a proper wife and he fulfills his original plan. Petruchio's determined persistence brings him success, both personal and financial. Everyone wins.

John Kelly faced disasters that, though less personal, were likewise daunting. When he became president of Pak Mail Centers of America in 1989, the franchised chain of packaging and shipping stores was losing $1.2 million per year. Kelly quickly closed the company's fifty weakest stores, following the prescription of the gardener in *Richard II:* "Superfluous branches we lop away, that bearing boughs may live." The one hundred thirty-five franchises "bearing boughs" were pushed to market themselves more effectively, and soon the company began to expand again. Today there are more than three hundred and fifty franchises worldwide; fifty-three were awarded in the U.S. in 1998.

Growth of the publicly traded company continues to be strong for the fourth consecutive year. Because of increases in royalty income and franchise fees, as well as careful attention to operating costs and support for each franchisee, Pak Mail's net income rose by a staggering 127 percent in the fiscal year ending November 30, 1998.

LESSON FOUR

"Your eyes advance after your thoughts."

—the Chorus, in *Henry V*

Corporate executives must establish firm, clear vision to provide company direction and inspiration. Otherwise navigation becomes tricky. Lacking a clear goal, the organization never knows if it is getting where it needs to go.

While Henry doesn't have the luxury of a policy-planning staff and off-site strategizing meetings, he proves himself a great leader in identifying and then pursuing a clear vision. He shows stunning imagination by transforming his seemingly insurmountable military liabilities into startling assets.

Richard of Gloucester, later to become the dastardly Richard III, best described this kind of vision in *Henry VI, Part III*. He compared a great leader to someone who "stands upon a promontory and spies a far-off shore where he would tread, wishing his foot were equal with his eye," someone who "chides the sea that sunders him from thence, saying he'll lade it dry to have his way."

President John F. Kennedy had a similarly far-reaching vision in May 1961, when he pledged that America would land a man on the moon by that decade's end. In those nascent days of space travel, the endeavor was fraught with recognized and unknown risks. Still, the President set the goal, unapologetically. "We do these things not because they are easy," he intoned, "but because they are hard."

This stirring philosophy applies equally to the heads

of today's fast-moving companies, well symbolized by Amazon.com. When Jeff Bezos read a report projecting annual growth of Web sales at 2,300 percent in 1994, the Princeton graduate conjured up the notion of a new company in a new industry. Quitting his job as senior vice president at D. E. Shaw, a hedge-fund firm, Bezos, along with wife MacKenzie and their golden retriever, drove west. On the way to Seattle he wrote the business plan for what was to become Amazon.com. Five days later, in their rented house in Bellevue, Washington, they opened their new business in their garage. Jeff Bezos created a clear vision of speeding up consumer access to products that "inspire, educate, and entertain." He states that, "once you have the big vision, you'll see that within it there are hundreds of smaller ones. You need the ability to do brutal triage, to be able to say, 'No, we don't do this and that. We're going to focus exclusively on these three things.' What is essential to success is consistently articulating the vision of what is to be achieved. You can have the best people, but if they're not all moving toward the same vision, it's not going to work."

Michael Dell, the thirty-four-year-old founder of Dell Computer, fits Valentine's description in *The Two Gentlemen of Verona:* "His years but young, but his experience old: his head unmellowed, but his judgment ripe." As a nineteen-year-old freshman at the University of Texas, Dell borrowed $1,000 from his parents to start a company that sold computer accessories out of his dorm room. Then he had the idea of making computers to order and selling them directly to consumers.

Dell performed much as the Bastard prescribes in *King John:* "Be great in act, as you have been in thought." He has rarely strayed from the vision that has been the growth engine of his company.

Dell's company sales grew 87 percent annually for the first eight years; since 1992 they've grown 55 percent annually. With $18.2 billion in revenue for fiscal 1999 and a market capitalization of about $108 billion, Dell Computer is now the leading company in direct sales of computers worldwide. It has established a powerful niche by customizing its products and services to consumers' requirements. In 1999, the company was ranked 78 in the Fortune 500.

LESSON FIVE

"There is occasions and causes,
and why and wherefore in all things"
—Fluellen, in *Henry V*

While displaying great courage and gazing far off for vision, a corporate leader must also look closely at critical small factors.

Just as paying scrupulous attention to detail helped King Henry achieve his ambitious goal, Russ Smith's keen interest in detail proved critical to his success. Smith, the editor and entrepreneur who created *New York Press* in 1988, now finds his free weekly paper to have 115,000 readers, encroaching on the 250,000 readership of its chief competitor, the *Village Voice.* Many observers believe that his launch pushed the

Voice into its 1996 decision to distribute papers for free in Manhattan.

Smith's interest in detail includes making regular forays through various New York City neighborhoods and "walking around reading and looking at every new publication, no matter how small or fringe it seems," he says. "Even if they're selling a full-page ad for two hundred dollars, I've got to keep telling myself that's two hundred dollars the *Press* should be competing for." His keen eyeballing pays off. His company currently generates an estimated $10 million in revenue annually.

Likewise, when Tom O'Keefe decided to open branches of his Seattle-based company, Tully's Coffee, in Asia, he took careful notice of local coffee-drinking traditions. What he discovered was that in places like Tokyo, most customers prefer to enjoy their beverage in a coffee shop or the privacy of their own offices. Downing java on the run to work was not their cup of tea. As a result, few potential customers saw the logos that appeared on his cups.

To get out his message while observing cultural nuances, O'Keefe, along with a couple of colleagues, drink coffee in front of one his shops. "We stand out front and drink two or three cups to show it's chic to carry Tully's Coffee on the street," he stated.

Striving to be number two in size but number one in quality in the eyes of his patrons, he opened Tully's Coffee stores across the street from his archrival, Starbuck's. His attention to detail has won him many customers. Tully's Coffee announced record growth for the fiscal year that ended in March 1998. Retail and wholesale growth increased 66 percent over the prior year, and comparable store sales were up by 14 percent over the prior year. Today, the chain has eighty-one locations in the U.S. and Asia.

LESSON SIX

"We will hear, note, and believe in heart
that what you speak is in your conscience."

—King Henry V

Executives must encourage straight talk and listen carefully, no matter how unpleasant the news.

People, as Henry appreciated, are an organization's most critical asset, the very key to victory. When Henry disguises his royal self and strolls among his men the night before battle, he gives them and especially himself a rare crucial opportunity by listening to them "speak in conscience." Because he takes the time to find out what his men are really thinking, he taps into their innate courage and turns their moods around the next day in his unforgettable St. Crispin's Day speech.

Listening well paid rewards for AOL as well. Candice Carpenter consulted for America Online in 1995, when the Internet company was trying to move from charging customers by the hour to a flat-rate subscription service. Company executives knew they would then need to sell more advertising to keep sales growing. Creating new content to attract advertisers was how AOL wanted to do it.

Carpenter, honest and straightforward, told them their efforts weren't well focused. She suggested instead that they create separate companies within AOL that could create content and become brands in their own right.

The executives, instead of throwing up barriers to contrary opinions, took the stance of Brutus in *Julius Caesar*: "What you have said, I will consider. What you have to say, I will with patience hear, and answer such high things."

The AOL response was to ask Carpenter to form a management team to do what she proposed. Accepting the challenge, Carpenter developed iVillage.com, the popular Web network targeted to women's interests.

A monthly average of ninety million page views of the site was recorded in the first quarter of 1999. Its first quarter revenue was $6.5 million, up an astounding 194 percent over the same period the year before. Not content to stop there, the company has formed strategic alliances with AOL, NBC, and AT&T. And its success has spawned a number of other Web sites for women who, according to iVillage's researchers, make up nearly half of all Internet users.

LESSON SEVEN

"Let my deeds be witness of my worth."

—Aaron, in *Titus Andronicus*

Executives need basic competence in the company's field of activity. Charisma and effort alone won't get the job done.

Basic competence is so fundamental to leadership that it's all too often forgotten. In *Henry V,* the noblemen and clergy have been dubious about Henry's abilities; his youthful dalliances and relative inexperience inspired scant confidence. Little by little, however, they come to think, like the Duke in *The Merchant of Venice*, that they "never knew so young a body with so old a head."

One of the most revered forms of competence among leaders is judgment. Today's corporate boards prefer an executive with sound judgment to one with great brilliance for good reason. While there's nothing wrong with having both, as Henry surely had, the law of conservation of good fortune seems to spread such attributes among us mere mortals in varying quantities, with more of this and less of that. It's rare for one individual to be blessed with both inspired creativity and the ability to deal steadily with the daily decisions of ongoing business. Or as Iago says in *Othello*, "We cannot all be masters," and even the finest executive cannot master all of the complex demands of his position.

Getting things done with high efficiency and low cost is business as usual for Sharon Anderson Wright of Half Price Books, even when pulling back is necessary. Since 1996, when she took over the Dallas-based company from its founder (her mother), she has grown the chain into a string of sixty-one bookstores by relying on the expertise of her personnel.

Her approach is simply to grow slowly without taking on risky and costly debt. As the Duchess of York says in *Richard III*, "Sweet flowers are slow, and weeds make haste." While Half Price Books opens only a few stores a year, it makes sure that they're successful.

Half Price, which sells new and used titles, keeps down costly mistakes by hiring managers for new stores exclusively from the ranks of seasoned employees. If the company wants to open a store in a new city but no experienced manager is available, it won't make the move.

Also, rather than invest in costly new construction, the chain rents existing space of all shapes and sizes. The original store, for example, was once a laundromat. Because renovations can be costly, the company runs its own woodshop. Where salaries are concerned, Wright does right by her team. None of the executives, including Wright herself, has a base salary exceeding $90,000 a year. Their love of books and of big challenges gives them motivation and satisfaction. As Antony says in *Antony and Cleopatra,* "To business that we love, we rise betime and go to it with delight."

To maintain the loyalty of her people, Wright offers a benefits package comparable to those at Border's and Barnes & Noble, as well as returning a portion of the company's earnings in a profit-sharing plan. Incentive is built in since the shares are based on the chain's performance in a given year. So far, the news is very good. Half Price Books expects to bring in $70 million in sales this year, up from $50 million in 1996.

Crate & Barrel is another example of a company where top managers carefully correlate growth with the expertise of staff available to them. Crate & Barrel, which had $530 million in sales in 1998 and 18 percent sales growth, could easily have gone public and thereby generated a huge windfall for its owners. With more than eighty stores nationwide, the chain is one of the hottest home furnishings retailers.

Thanks to a new Web site where consumers can orders its products, the company is poised to keep growing. But Crate & Barrel is only willing to open new stores in areas where it can attract the right staff. "To climb steep hills requires slow pace at first," Norfolk says in *Henry VIII*. This translates into a slow-growth formula that has seen four to eight new stores a year. "This is the way the company's management team puts excellence first," says CEO Gordon Segal. "We'd rather be the best than the biggest."

Today, managers often mistake strength in one realm for competence in another. The popular management philosophy of the sixties, that a good executive can manage anything, has largely been discredited. While a good manager can learn to manage almost anything, he or she still needs to have, or quickly acquire, the fundamental skills and knowledge of the company's product, market, and operations. A top IBM executive, for example, had better have a different idea of a mouse than does the head of an extermination company like the Victor Corporation or, for that matter, than Disney's Michael Eisner.

Michael Jordan is a prime example. Although no one has ever played better on the basketball court, the superathlete showed minimal competence on the professional baseball diamond. Jordan could get few products to endorse and advertise when he was wearing long pants and cleats, but had no trouble when wearing shorts and sneakers.

Similarly, Horatio, Hamlet's dear friend, may be competent as a sage but he fails dismally at most everything else. Among other tasks, he's asked to address the Ghost ("Thou art a scholar; speak to it, Horatio," the guard Marcellus orders) and get it to speak back, mark the King's reaction during the play within the play, and watch over an increasingly insane Ophelia. Horatio flubs nearly every assignment.

Several powerful residents of Elsinore besides Hamlet, including King Claudius and Queen Gertrude, all mistake Horatio's polished manner and reputation as a scholar as an indication of competence in accomplishing critical tasks.

Michael Dell learned to stick with what he knows the hard way. In 1991, when the company deviated from its effective direct selling to customers and tried to sell merchandise through computer superstores and warehouse clubs, sales suffered. The experiment was canceled.

Today, Dell wouldn't consider expanding beyond the computer industry. "I've learned from experience that a company can grow too fast," he says. "You have to be careful about expanding into new businesses because if you get into too many too quickly, you won't have the experience or the infrastructure to succeed."

This is one of the hardest lessons in judgment for a burgeoning new business to accept. Overreaching in a surprisingly boundless market is one of the more common causes of failure among startup companies. Overly optimistic sales forecasts, excessive borrowing, and overexpanded plants are the symptoms to watch for.

LESSON EIGHT

"Do what honor would thee do."

—the Chorus, in *Henry V*

A great corporate leader cares deeply about the team. Henry set the standard on "the way things are done around here" by showing concern for his troops and dedication to his mission. As a result, he inspired both personal loyalty and extraordinary performance among the team as a whole.

Employees' sense of service to the company comes primarily from the example of top management. But it can be reinforced by having a corporate credo. To assure that all employees know what's expected of them, management must decide and explain what it wants. If top executives handle their positions masterfully, the sentiment of both employees and customers toward the company's leaders can echo another King Henry (*Henry VI, Part II*), who confessed, "I thank them for their tender loving care."

Business leaders who conduct themselves with integrity and concern for employees triumph, even in daunting situations. For instance, after Jeff Polep sold his father's company, J. Polep Distribution Services, to Trade Development Corp. in 1984, he watched in horror as that Texas-based enterprise filed for Chapter 11. The business where his great-grandfather and grandfather worked, which had delivered candy, cigarettes, and groceries to retail stores for more than one hundred years, was dissolving before his eyes.

That wasn't all. When he sold the company, he was

named president, which entailed signing a noncompete agreement for the term of his employment and five years afterward if he quit. Once TDC filed for bankruptcy, the company refused to fire him and thus relieve him of his obligation.

Determined to save his family's company, Polep traveled to Amarillo, Texas, where the bankruptcy case had been filed, and waited determinedly on the courthouse steps for a week until he could get his case heard. The judge was succinct: TDC was ordered to either pay him or fire him.

Polep succeeded: He was fired.

Then free to start his own business, Polep did so with the positive, forward-looking attitude of Richard II: "Deep malice makes too deep incision." Polep followed the King's advice: "Forget, forgive: conclude and be agreed."

He began by calling former employees who had been loyal to him. A small group agreed to work for him, without pay, for the first sixty days. Next he opened an office and began trying to win back his old suppliers. Stunned by TDC's bankruptcy, they didn't exactly welcome him with open arms.

Still, by drawing on what Mowbray in *Richard II* calls a "spotless reputation," Polep was gradually able to win the support necessary to rebuild the business. One manufacturer personally guaranteed some of the loans he sorely needed, and a friend loaned him a million dollars.

Two months later, his old building was released by the bank. With the help of fifty people, he embarked on an aggressive sales plan. Today the company has more than two hundred employees; in 1998 it brought in $180 million.

Not surprisingly, those who set the tone for caring about people and fulfilling the mission inspire others throughout the organization to do likewise. One of Shakespeare's most inspiring warriors, Hotspur is, as his name implies, hot-tempered. At any moment's notice, he is ready, in *Henry IV, Part I,* to tie on his spurs and charge into battle.

Once on the battlefield, he stirs his comrades with his fierce fighting. The bigger the challenge, the more he relishes it.

So inspiringly courageous is Hotspur that his foil, Prince Hal, jealously mocks him, saying that Hotspur boasts that he "kills me some six or seven dozen of Scots at a breakfast, washes his hands, and says to his wife, 'Fie upon this quiet life! I want work.'"

Hal's father, King Henry IV, holds a more admiring and indeed accurate view of the warrior. He says of Hotspur, "He turns head against the lion's armed jaw, and leads ancient lord and . . . reverend Bishops on to bloody battles and to bruising arms. What never-dying honour hath he got!" Summing up, he calls Hotspur a "Mars in swathling clothes, this infant warrior, [who] in his enterprises" defeats great foes and inspires the entire army. Hotspur shows "how things were done around" there on the battlefield.

Being tough helped Amber Brookman, the marketing director of Coated Sales, a textile-manufacturing business in New York City. Arriving at work one day in May

1988, she learned that most of the company's top officers had been accused of accounting fraud. Brookman, who was also an officer but had nothing to do with the financial side of the company, took charge.

Because she didn't know finance, she had to hire experts to examine the company's books. A month after the alleged fraud, she had a lawyer put the company into Chapter 11 bankruptcy protection. This bought her time to reorganize the company and put creditors on hold until she could figure out a way to pay them. In the meantime the company looked for a buyer, shuttered some of its divisions, and reduced expenses. "It was depressing, embarrassing, and frightening," Brookman recalls.

Finally, in 1989, she managed to sell the company's assets to The Hallwood Group, Inc., a holding company in Dallas. Named president and CEO, Brookman's solid leadership has paid off. She helped the new owners reopen the company under the name Brookwood Companies. Sales at The Hallwood Group, which derives more than half of its revenue from Brookwood Companies, reached $116.3 million in 1998, up from $40.9 million in 1995. "We stayed the course through the crisis," Brookman says. "A lot of the good people have stayed."

A true leader stresses ethics constantly in both word and deed. In modern corporations, the CEO and top staff must set the standard by being "armed so strong in honesty," as Brutus says, that they follow the right road. "Honor travels in a strait so narrow," Ulysses says in *Troilus and Cressida,* "where but one goes abreast. Keep, then, the path."

Great leaders know what they stand for and why. They set and show the organization's moral compass by talking right and walking the talk. Ronald Reagan put the point nicely:

> The character that takes command in moments of crucial choices has already been determined—by a thousand other choices made earlier in seemingly unimportant moments—by all those "little" choices of years past—by all those times when the voice of conscience was at war with the voice of temptation— whispering a lie that "it doesn't really matter"—by all the day-to-day decisions made when life seemed easy and crises seemed far away, the decisions that piece by piece, bit by bit, developed habits of discipline or of laziness; habits of self-sacrifice, or self-indulgence; habits of duty and honor and integrity— or dishonor and shame.

What Reagan stated with characteristic eloquence, Shakespeare said with characteristic pith in *Two Gentlemen of Verona:* "How use doth breed a habit in a man!"

President Reagan also had a small sign on his Oval Office desk that read, THERE'S NO LIMIT TO WHAT A MAN CAN DO, OR WHERE HE CAN GO, IF HE DOESN'T MIND WHO GETS THE CREDIT. (Corporate wags transformed his lesson into: An honest executive is one who shares credit with the people who did all the work. Or the two kinds of leaders are those interested in the flock and those interested in the fleece.)

True leaders bring out the best in those around them, as in themselves. They transform ordinary people into extraordinary achievers. They turn run-of-the-mill companies into productive and profitable institutions.

Upon the values and performance of leaders depends the contribution of many others, as Rosencrantz in *Hamlet* reminds King Claudius: "The single and peculiar" lives of ordinary people are given meaning through their own individual thinking. But no leader acts alone. Rather, "like a gulf doth draw what's near it with it. It is a massy wheel fixed on the summit of the highest mount, to whose huge spokes ten thousand lesser things are mortised and adjoined." When the leader "falls, each small" part "attends the boist'rous ruin."

And when the leader does succeed, he or she succeeds for the great benefit of all and thereby engenders the kind of awe that even the conspirator Cassius realizes was present in the personage of Julius Caesar: "Why, man, he doth bestride the narrow world like a Colossus, and we petty men walk under his huge legs and peep about."

ACT II

CONFRONTING CHANGE

"O Brave New World,

That Has Such People in It!"

[DRAMATIS EXECUTIVUS SUMMARIUS]

"What's new?" This is the striking question Shakespeare employs, one way or another, to begin each of his plays. Business executives should begin every day with the same question.

The Bard understood fast change. Some episodic event—usually unwelcome, always tricky to handle—launches most of his dramas. From there, circumstances take strange twists and turns, but in the midst of these changes, Shakespeare's protagonists exude the same sense of awe expressed by Miranda in *The Tempest* and quoted above. And most of them grow in ability and insight. They learn and adjust so completely that they leave the stage very different people from when they first appeared, much like Prince Hal, in *Henry IV, Part II,* who says, smartly, "Presume not that I am the thing I was."

We don't presume that about any Shakespearean characters—especially Petruchio, costar of *The Taming of the Shrew.* Brimming with wit, optimism, and imagination, he's one of Shakespeare's best-loved characters. He's also a model for today's corporate executive who must initiate, guide, and deal with change.

Today, constantly shifting markets, products, and problems force corporate executives to cope with the winds of change and manage fast-breaking situations for customers, shareholders, and employees as best they can. Fixed in their goals, executives must stay flexible in their means.

The story of Petruchio, both a victim and an agent of dramatic change, offers useful advice for inundated executives who wonder, "How am I ever going to cope with this much change?"

PROLOGUE

Flamboyant, creative Petruchio is thrust into a new situation by a sudden turn of events he neither expected nor wanted, namely his father's death. In response, he is bold and decisive, seizing on the new opportunities that arise. He settles on a long-term goal, opens it to challenge, and then, having weighed the pros and cons, sticks by it. His implementation is as meticulous as it is flexible.

As with any effective corporate executive, some of

his plans don't pan out. Indeed, Petruchio's first strategy fails and has to be replaced by a backup scheme, one that is far tougher to implement.

Still, so many things go right that his success is stunning. While he comes to Padua to do well, he leaves Padua doing good. In effect, he changes the life of a miserable young woman and her wretched household, and he rocks traditions in their stagnant society. In the course of all this, Petruchio gains more than he could ever have dreamed.

Scene I

[Enter young man, filled with energy and looking for ventures, into a new town]

Petruchio bursts into Padua exclaiming, "Antonio my father is deceased." Undeterred by sadness, he fixes on his assets, asserting, "My fortune lives for me." He follows the advice of Cymbeline: "Be cheerful. Wipe thine tears. Some falls are means the happier to arise."

Itching to get going, he joins that caravan of "young men [scattered] through the world to seek their fortunes farther than at home, where small experience grows."

In seeking his fortune, Petruchio makes some shrewd executive moves. First, he establishes a clear goal. Though young and wild, he will not go careening aimlessly. Second, in venturing beyond his hometown, he decides to stay in familiar territory. He travels from Verona to Padua, not to Bolivia or Patagonia. Like any sound executive, he senses that what works well in one market may not succeed in a different one. It is risky enough to change the product line; to compound the risk by simultaneously changing the customer base invariably courts disaster. Third, he has assessed a core competency, namely wooing Italian women with wealthy fathers. Putting all this together, he establishes as his goal to "wive it wealthily in Padua—If wealthily, then happily in Padua."

So, Petruchio has defined his market (Padua), his product (himself), and his potential source of capital (a dowry-adorned maiden). He even has a ready-made customer base: the elite of the town.

Thus to one such wealthy father does he go. Baptista, a member of the gentry of Padua, realizes that he needs change as well. His daughters have come of age, but he is trapped by social convention. He must "not . . . bestow my youngest daughter before I have a husband for the elder."

That youngest daughter, Bianca, yearns for marriage and attracts a gaggle of suitors but resigns herself to having only "my books and [musical] instruments" as her "company, on them to look and practice by myself."

Her older sister, Katherine, is also trapped and alone. Unmanageable and unbearable, the lovely Katherine acts ugly. She's the shrew to be tamed.

Petruchio is determined to marry the wealthy Katherine, but like any good executive, he carefully listens to objections to setting his goal too high. Hortensio, one of Bianca's suitors, emphatically states that Katherine's behavior is "beyond all measure, that were my state far worser than it is, I would not wed her for a mine of gold." Petruchio, however, counters that Hortensio "knowest not gold's effect."

When Gremio, another of Bianca's suitors, asks if Petruchio knows "all her faults," our hero makes it clear that, like any good manager, he has assessed the situation carefully. "I know she is an irksome brawling scold," Petruchio brags with that boundless confidence executives need most in tough situations. "If that be all, masters, I hear no harm."

Petruchio boasts that he's been through worse situations than hearing a woman shrieking at him. "Think you a little din can daunt mine ears? Have I not in my time heard lions roar?" He brags that "a woman's tongue" thus isn't anything more to him than "a chestnut" popping "in a farmer's fire."

Petruchio's brass and brains intrigue Bianca's suitors. Hortensio even proposes that he and Gremio bankroll Petruchio's expenses in wooing Katherine, so that her sister Bianca can be freed for their courting. Gremio readily agrees, but only on a strictly "success fee only" basis: "And so we will, provided that he win her." This may well have been one of the earliest uses of contingency fees in contracting.

Before even meeting Katherine, Petruchio makes some key decisions. First, although in Padua as a victim of change, he'll take advantage of his new situation. Second, he himself will become an agent of change. Petruchio refuses a phony marriage with Katherine simply as a ploy to get the dowry, and he will not live with her as she is. Therefore he decides that he must force fundamental changes: He must tame the shrew.

As in any business acquisition the key question is not what is being bought, but rather what will the purchase become?

Confident of his scheme, Petruchio calls on Baptista in his villa with a hearty, "And you, good sir! Pray, have you not a daughter called Katherina, fair and virtuous?" An honest gentleman, Baptista replies resignedly, "I have a daughter, sir, called Katherina."

The subject of their exchange, Katherine, needs change more than anybody else, for she is ensnared by strong forces. Unequal by convention to men who, like Petruchio, can leave home to seek their fate, she's confined to her father's villa in Padua until a husband takes control over her life.

Moreover, her father confines Katherine by insisting that marriage order follow birth order. And he understandably favors Bianca, because Bianca is agreeable while her sister is an "intolerable curst." Yet this evident partiality pains Katherine, who spews to her father: "*She* is your treasure. *She* must have a husband," while Katherine must live alone and humiliated. Had her father been a more astute businessman, he might have foreseen the dangers of favoring one daughter while overlooking the greater potential of her more difficult-to-manage sister. His behavior is a common failing among businessmen when dealing with product lines, subordinates, and even customers.

Still, the most significant factor holding Katherine back is her own personality. While she acts appallingly to her family and visitors alike, she is most wounding to herself. Dysfunctional and seemingly incapable of love or of even connecting with anyone else, Katherine stands isolated in her misery, too troubled to attract suitors, take music lessons, sit and read a book, or open her mind for education. (Petruchio later picks up on this theme; the entire play embodies Katherine's education.)

Katherine's outlet is rage. Her tirades mask her keen wit, strong will, and teeming life force, attributes suppressed by Paduan social convention. Her outsize personality is in fact a good match for Petruchio. He wants to wrap up this business fast so that he can get on with his new life. The quintessence of a young man in a hurry, he embodies many of the qualities of fine salesmen: perseverance, energy, and a total inability to accept the word *no*.

Scene II

[Enter wild-eyed woman, hair and dress amiss, with young man laughing uproariously.]

Unbeknownst to Katherine, Petruchio has developed an innovative plan, which he lays out in considerable detail. He will "woo her with some spirit when she comes," using positive reinforcement by treating her not as she *is*, but as she *should be*. This is a smart business plan since people tend to respond as they are treated. When employees are doubted they become cautious; when applauded they become energetic.

Hence, Petruchio will regard Katherine as if she were tender and treat her with kindness. As he explains, if she shrilly scolds him, he'll respond with calm coos. If she were to "rail, why then I'll tell her plain she sings as sweetly as a nightingale." If she asks him to leave, he'll thank her for welcoming him; if she dismisses the possibility of marriage, he'll discuss exchanging rings and setting their wedding day.

His overall approach thus carefully set forth, he begins to implement it when they meet. His first words to her are "Good morrow, Kate." She suggests that he is deaf since "they call me Katherine that do talk of me."

Not Petruchio. To win his point, Petruchio calls her Kate ten times in rapid succession, usually with flattering adjectives attached. Other people may call her "plain Kate," but he considers her "the prettiest Kate in Christendom." Among those in the know, her "mildness [is] praised in every town" and her virtues celebrated widely. That's why he's "moved to woo thee for my wife."

A major element in Petruchio's audacious restructuring plan is renaming her. It's a stunning gambit but an approach backed by solid theory. Not only executives, but also parents, teachers, and coaches understand Petruchio's principle: When you expect more, you get more.

After they engage in rapid-fire verbal combat and chase each other around a bit, Katherine suddenly strikes him. This immediately and fundamentally alters their first encounter. "I swear I'll cuff you if you strike again," Petruchio threatens. Though it's hard to penetrate her psychic defenses on most matters, Katherine understands that Petruchio means business here. As any sage businessperson must know, there comes a time to lay down the law. But, as Shakespeare teaches, this can be done only rarely—and only at the pivotal moment.

Petruchio continues praising her and bluntly reveals his intentions: "I am . . . born to tame you, Kate, and bring you from a wild Kate to a Kate . . . conformable as other household Kates." He conveys his big news: "In plain terms: your father hath consented that you shall be my wife, your dowry agreed on, and will you, nill you, I will marry you." This take-all attitude is a worthy external pose in many business situations such as when a firm must deter a potential interloper from entering a market or engage in a hostile bidding contest for an acquisition. Confidence and the show of confidence count for a lot.

For Katherine this is grossly unfair, since she had no say in the deal; she is merely being passed from one man to another, like a certificate of common stock, without her knowledge or consent.

Yet Petruchio also speaks of her worth to him. There's no gaming when he says, "Thy beauty doth make me like thee well." Before going further, he catches himself to end their private meeting with, "Thou must be married to no man but me," as if there could be another contender.

To Baptista and the fellows, Petruchio boasts how he and Katherine "have agreed so well together that upon Sunday is the wedding day." She has not agreed and is furious. She says she'd rather "see thee hanged on Sunday next."

Petruchio heads for Venice to prepare for their wedding. His parting words are: "Kiss me, Kate."

Despite his playfulness and cockeyed optimism, Petruchio remains realistic. One of the toughest challenges for an executive is to outwardly exude confidence while inwardly weighing new facts and changing odds. To do otherwise can produce exactly the outcome he is trying to avoid. Still, Petruchio's first approach, consisting of positive verbal reinforcement, yields disappointing results. Katherine is unchanged. On the road to Venice, Petruchio must therefore conduct a midcourse review. Despite his carefully thought out, well-executed plan, a talking cure just won't suffice.

Before his return to Padua, Petruchio must devise another approach if his goal is to be met.

SCENE III

[Enter young man dressed like a clown and acting like a madman.]

Theirs is a most unusual wedding but, then again, they are a most unusual couple.

Violating the first rule of a business meeting, Petruchio inexplicably arrives hours late for his own wedding, and when he does arrive the bride's father wishes he hadn't come at all. Petruchio turns up dressed like a clown and proceeds to act like an idiot. Then he abducts the bride before their wedding feast even begins. Petruchio's backup plan thus gets under way. This approach focuses on negative action.

At this point Petruchio carefully reviews where his project stands, reminding himself that he began by being gentle ("Thus have I politically begun my reign") and is adamant to achieve his goal and "end successfully." He explains that this new plan entails training Katherine like one of his falcons. He will deprive her of food and sleep and "make her come and know her keeper's call." Such deprivation may jolt her psyche and open her awareness of how one's behavior affects others. He will find "some undeserved fault" and generally act dysfunctional himself.

This seems cruel, but it "is done in reverend care of her. . . . This is a way to kill a wife with kindness." After explaining his two-pronged approach, Petruchio takes the wise management step of asking if anyone else has anything better in mind. Hearing no other options, he proceeds to phase two.

The newlyweds leave Padua for Petruchio's place in Verona. There Petruchio beats his valet, screams at his household staff, overturns the dining table covered with food he claims is burnt, and shreds dresses the tailor has brought to show Katherine. Out of Katherine's hearing, he makes amends, such as paying the tailor for the torn clothes.

Petruchio's extreme measures are meant to compel change and, despite all his craziness, Petruchio stays focused. One of his servants nearly grasps what he's up to when commenting, "He kills her in her own humor." After knocking a pitcher from a servant's hand and screaming at him, "You whoreson villain, will you let it fall?" Petruchio hits the poor lad. Katherine immediately intervenes and tells Petruchio, "Patience, I pray you, 'twas a fault unwilling."

Petruchio's mirrorlike behavior shows Kate that she can still be spirited and rebellious—such is her nature—

51

but that she must also be psychologically and socially functional and loving. The falcon, after training, doesn't become a parakeet; it's still strong, smart, and a bit wild, but its actions are purposeful and appropriate to its kind.

When she fancies one of the tailor's caps and tells Petruchio she'll have it because "this doth fit the time and gentlewomen wear such caps as these," he retorts, "When you are gentle, you shall have one, too—and not till then."

Similarly, executives are often unable to earn the mantle of respect because they cannot see themselves as others see them. By the time someone points out their behavior, it is often too late. It is far better to accept a truthful personal assessment.

Petruchio, ever the good executive, test markets his new approach as he proceeds. When the pair leave Verona to return to Padua, he remarks, "How bright and goodly shines the moon!" She points out, "The sun. It is not moonlight now." He says moon, she says sun until Petruchio starts to turn back, declaring, "It shall be moon or star or what I list, Or ere I journey to your father's house." In the face of this threat, she suddenly turns cooperative, agreeing, "Be it moon or sun or what you please." His plan seems to be working. On the road to Padua, he tests her further by asking for a kiss in public. Katherine is compliant, and for the first time calls him "love." Petruchio then comments with kindness, "Is not this well? Come, my sweet Kate." He's grateful for her first consensual sign of affection, declaring, "Better once than never, for never too late."

Kate's transformation becomes public in the final test, when, after Bianca weds in secret, Baptista throws his second wedding feast. After the meal, the ladies retire while the men drink and carouse, as custom dictates.

But Petruchio doesn't live by custom. Having radically changed Katherine's character, he now seeks to change social convention by ending the separation of the sexes. After some of the men brag about their wives, he proposes a wager. Petruchio says that each should send for his wife and "whose wife is most obedient to come at first when he doth send for her shall win the wager."

Bianca and another woman refuse to obey. Petruchio then summons Kate. She comes bursting in. "What is your will, sir," she inquires with a flourish, "that you send for me?" He dispatches her back to fetch the other women.

As requested, Kate returns with them. Then, to these disobedient wives, their husbands, her father, her husband, and everyone else, Kate delivers the play's longest and most polished speech on a wife's duty to her husband. This, one of Shakespeare's most controversial speeches, contains pockets of mockery and is so exaggerated in both its style and message that it need not be taken at face value.

Winning the wager and delivering such a discourse upstages her sister Bianca at her own wedding party. In the play's opening scenes, Katherine had everyone's attention; by its closing scene, she has both attention and approval.

By now Kate understands how dramatically Petruchio has changed her. Now she can deliver the disquisition as a gift in return for his healing powers and love. She specifically mentions "so great a debt" a wife owes her husband.

The instant she finishes her verbal extravaganza Petruchio leaps up ecstatically, crying, "Why, there's a wench! Come on and kiss me, Kate!" which she most passionately does. Finally he seeks another kind of play with his partner: "Come, Kate, we'll to bed." Off they go to consummate, at last, their now-real marriage.

Their spirits merged, Kate and Petruchio become the most compatible couple in all of Shakespeare. Change has enabled them to live together, happily ever after. And Petruchio's careful plan—articulated in several stages—is shown to be supremely successful.

ACTING LESSONS

Petruchio's method of handling change in a creative and determined manner furnishes six critical lessons on seizing opportunities, grasping future potential, staying in familiar territory, forcing change, moving fast, and becoming nimble.

LESSON ONE

"I could heartily wish this had not befallen; but
since it is as it is, mend it for your own good."

—Iago, in *Othello*

Turning misfortunes into opportunities becomes even more crucial in our times, when change in the business world arrives at breakneck speed.

The inability of companies to recognize, and then leap on, new opportunities knocks some 7 percent of Fortune 500 companies off that prized list each year. While some firms and industries do ride the stormy winds of change on to promising new endeavors, others succumb to the ill winds. Corporate history is filled with once-dominant companies like Pan Am or Penn Central Railroad that could not adapt fast enough to their radically changed markets. Others, like IBM, General Motors, and AT&T, have experienced near-misses. Still, many businesses like America Online, Amazon.com, and eBay are managing to traverse today's information highway at unimaginable speeds. For others, the consumer jury is still out. Eastman Kodak, a company at the top of its field for years, is suddenly seeing its specializations in chemistry and film increasingly threatened by electronics and microchips.

At the beginning of the century, nearly all of the ten largest American firms were in the business of extracting natural resources. As the century closes, America's ten largest companies are primarily hi-tech, leading-edge firms. The only company to appear on both lists is the ever-adapting General Electric Co.

Many changes are unsettling, and some hit at a deeply personal level, like the death of Petruchio's father. In the words of Paulina in *The Winter's Tale,* "What's gone and what's past help should be past grief."

While dealing with his grief, Petruchio also seizes the opportunities it opens to him.

Bill Lederer took a similar approach when his father developed cancer. Leaving his successful Wall Street career in 1997, Lederer returned to his family's framing and art supplies business. Soon he and his wife moved the framing business to the Internet, where they launched ArtUframe.com. Later, the name was changed to Art.com when it became an online poster and print shop.

In early June 1999, Getty Images, the giant firm that owns a group of stock-photo and film-footage businesses, bought Art.com for $84 million in cash and 4.5 million shares of Getty Images stock, then worth about $200 million.

This ability to transform a tragedy into an opportunity is a hallmark of winners. Prospero, the hero of *The Tempest,* rules as the Duke of Milan until his brother Antonio and his cadre overthrows his reign. Prospero, along with his infant daughter Miranda, is set adrift on a rickety raft. Surviving against all odds, they land on a tropical island. With the help of the spirit Ariel and the quasibarbaric Caliban, Prospero builds a new life. His lovely daughter, magical powers, and beloved books—"my library was dukedom large enough"—make him happy.

Years later, that same band of conspirators is suddenly shipwrecked on his island. Their dramatic appearance offers new opportunities for Prospero, which he seizes.

The board of USWeb, like Petruchio and Prospero,

turned a bad situation into something successful. News leaked out in November 1998 about the judgment abilities of Joe Firmage, the company's CEO and main visionary. It seems that his new book was a bit too visionary as it expressed Firmage's controversial ideas about time travel and life on other planets. The company's board acted quickly to avoid potential embarrassment by launching a rapid executive search.

Soon Firmage was replaced by Robert Shaw. A former executive at Oracle, Shaw helped the $50 million consulting business grow to a $2 billion company within six years. Today, USWeb Corp., known as USWeb/CKS after a merger with the interactive agency CKS Group, is one of a few dominant players in the Internet advertising business. It has regained lost ground, reporting record revenue for the first quarter of 1999. Sales were $84.1 million for the first quarter of 1999, up 16 percent over revenue for the prior quarter.

The 3M company likewise showed how to turn a major disappointment into a stunning success. Seeking to develop a new super-strength adhesive, top-notch 3M scientists discovered a "glue" that could barely hold on to itself, let alone anything else.

For years Dr. Spence Silver, the inventor of the glue, tried to win support for its use among his colleagues. Then one of those researchers, Art Fry, applied a small blob of that nonglue to a scrap of paper to mark the pages in his hymnal for the church choir. Before long, his choral colleagues requested markers of their own. Next, the scientist made small pads of sticky paper for the company secretaries, and, by 1981, a year after their introduction, the newly named Post-it notes flooded the marketplace.

Adversity can strike any industry, even such hardy perennials as the aerospace/defense business. In November 1989, the Berlin Wall fell, soon followed by the collapse of the Warsaw Pact, of the Soviet Union itself, and then of U.S. defense spending. This staggering domino effect occurred just as Martin Marietta, in the wake of surviving a hostile takeover attempt, was converting from a highly diversified commercial firm into a highly concentrated defense firm.

Within a few years, the domestic market for defense products fell by an astonishing 72 percent in real purchasing power, and the industry braced itself for two million layoffs.

Though the Duke Senior in *As You Like It* says, "Sweet are the uses of adversity, which, like the toad, ugly and venomous, wears yet a precious jewel in his head," many defense contractors had a tough time spotting any precious jewels during this period.

Nonetheless, the fundamental alteration of global conditions changed the dynamics of the situation and opened new opportunities. Previously bitter rivals now sat down to discuss what might be done. The formula for success was evident: Combine one company's half-utilized plant with the half-utilized plant of another, add a dose of synergy, and an efficient enterprise could be created.

This strategy of expansion was implemented time and again, much as the fisherman in the little-known Shakespeare play *Pericles* says: "The great ones eat up the little ones." Finally, the previously midsize Martin

Marietta became big enough to merge with the mighty Lockheed Corporation as an equal in 1995. Before long, seventeen leading defense firms, including General Electric Aerospace, General Dynamics Aircraft and Space, Loral, RCA Aerospace, IBM Federal Systems, and Goodyear Aerospace, had been consolidated under the Lockheed Martin banner.

All this activity produced the second largest company in its field and reaped enough efficiencies to avert ballooning fixed costs and to realize more than $2.6 billion in annual savings, which were shared with its customers. During a period when investors commonly forecasted the industry's collapse, Lockheed Martin stockholders enjoyed returns twice as brisk as the already brisk market gains during those years.

Before the U.S. defense budget collapse, none of these opportunities was open. After the dominos fell, however, among the most amazing outcomes was a highly lucrative partnership with a Russian firm to launch commercial telecommunication satellites. As Exeter says, when speaking to the French king about the personal transformation of Prince Hal to King Henry, "Be assured, you'll find a difference as we his subjects have in wonder found, between the promise of his greener days and these he masters now."

But just as change is disruptive to the old order, so is it rich with opportunity. When "discontinuities" strike, new businesses can sprout up without having to compete with an established company. These discontinuities, which may take the form of technological breakthroughs, regulatory changes, or a host of other transitions, are where the budding entrepreneur should look for startup opportunities.

LESSON TWO

"We know what we are, but not what we may be."

—Ophelia, in *Hamlet*

Battered by change from all sides as well as global forces, corporate executives must set a few clear goals, make them as creative and worthy as possible, proclaim them clearly, and stick with them until completion.

Petruchio could have joined that caravan of young men without any purpose, but he goes forth with a clear goal in mind that challenges and stretches him. Against all expectations and odds, he finally attains it.

Fernando Espuelas and Jack Chen, both thirty-two, set a demanding goal for themselves. When these former high-school buddies launched StarMedia, the largest Internet network in Latin America, in September 1996, they lacked the resources available to the bigger players like Yahoo and AOL. What they did have, however, was a clear and creative objective that was well timed and well executed.

Neither of the huge firms had tapped into the Latin American market. Doing some demographic research, Espuelas and Chen discovered that 20 percent of the population controlled 65 percent of the wealth in Central and South America. They concluded that 100 million people were likely to try the Web.

Ready to take the plunge, Espuelas, who had been a

managing director at AT&T, and Chen, who had worked as a securities manager at CS First Boston Investment Management, ponied up $100,000 in savings. This amount, together with another $400,000 raised from friends and family, allowed them to rent a decrepit house in Greenwich, Connecticut, and hire a small crew to design a Web site.

They did not consider themselves limited by their age or lack of resources. Rather, they followed the counsel of Helena in *All's Well That Ends Well:* "Our remedies oft in ourselves do lie, which we ascribe to heaven."

Their solution was to work around the clock to put up the site. Along the way they overcame big problems, including the resignation of their lead producer just a few weeks before the launch. By May of 1997, they had developed a forty-page business plan and were ready to approach venture capitalists for more money.

Soon they had convinced Fred Wilson, at Flatiron Partners, and Chase Capital Partners, both based in New York, to invest over $3.5 million. By bringing in these respected players, they shored up their credibility. Other investors—including David Rockefeller and Henry Kravis—followed, as did strategic partners such as Intel, GE Capital, and Morgan Stanley. In the largest round of private equity financing ever done by an Internet company to that point, StarMedia raised $80 million. The prospects for the future look bright. Market value soon reached $2.28 billion.

Even more impressive is the lead this gutsy company has taken over its potential competitors. Yahoo en español wasn't launched until June 1998, and AOL doesn't plan to begin operating its own Spanish language venture until the end of 1999.

LESSON THREE

"All difficulties are but easy
when they are known."
—Duke, in *Measure for Measure*

Executives who seek to expand their markets and/or products had best begin in fairly familiar territory. While the Duke may exaggerate a little—all hardships aren't easy, even when known—they are easier the more familiar they are. Petruchio ventures forth from Verona but stays on fairly familiar ground.

In the same way, today's executive should stick closely to the company's core competencies. The further afield management goes, the higher the failure rate.

Shifting business activities from one market to another or from one product line to another is extremely difficult. To try both simultaneously is downright hazardous. No management should change more than one major business variable at a time except as a last resort.

One of Shakespeare's greatest creations, Falstaff, fails to thrive when venturing too far afield. He is most magnificent at the earthy Boar's-Head Tavern with Prince Hal (the future King Henry V) and his rugged gang. He jokes, trains Hal on human nature, and instigates much commotion and amusement. Falstaff justifiably boasts, "I am not only witty in myself, but the cause that wit is in other men."

Yet when Falstaff ventures beyond what he knows well, his stock plummets. In sophisticated Windsor Falstaff is neither witty nor the cause of much wit in others. Having strayed too far, his sense of timing is somewhat off, his jokes fall flat, and his insights seem trivial.

Victoria's Secret is one company that learned the importance of sticking with its core competency. As the company's catalogs took off in the early nineties, the national lingerie retailer gradually branched out into products such as bathing suits and eveningwear. At the same time, executives started to neglect the product that had put the company on the map: its bras. By 1994, Sara Lee—a highly diversified company best known for its bakery division—was making a dent in Victoria's Secret's core business with its new WonderBra.

In the midst of an identity crisis by 1996, Victoria's Secret's sales went flat. That year, however, the company merged with a bigger firm, Intimate Brands, the parent company for Bath & Body Works. Leslie H. Wexner, the chairman of Intimate Brands, decided on a strategy posed by Posthumus in *Cymbeline,* who says, "I will begin the fashion—less without and more within" and so changed the company by offering the best bras on the market. Soon Victoria's Secret launched the Miracle Bra in an advertising blitz that featured high-profile models Claudia Schiffer and Tyra Banks.

By returning to its main strength, Victoria's Secret has seen big results. In 1998, Intimate Brands' sales reached $3.9 billion, a 56 percent increase over 1996. And, because the company focused on higher quality products, it was able to reduce discounts that had been shrinking its profit margins. Between 1997 and 1998 alone, the publicly traded company's net income rose to $400.2 million—$1.59 per share—a 21 percent jump. In the first six months of 1999 the stock price climbed 170 percent, to $51 a share.

Heinz is another company that has learned the same lesson the hard way. After realizing that it had become too large and complicated to operate efficiently, it recently announced a plan to focus more closely on its six core products and streamline other operations. Heinz plans to emphasize key products like ketchup, frozen foods, and tuna in the six countries that generate its greatest sales. Simultaneously it will trim the fat by shedding peripheral businesses such as Weight Watchers classes and by closing fifteen to twenty plants it deems inessential. Based on this plan, the company projects $200 million in annual savings by 2002.

LESSON FOUR

"Who would not change a raven for a dove?"

—Lysander, in A *Midsummer Night's Dream*

The best executives today encourage or force change, particularly in situations that do not immediately demand it. They overrule resistance from employees and others, especially during times of merger or acquisition, when many naysayers claim that the new units don't fit into the existing corporate culture.

There's a natural tendency to get comfortable when the established way of doing things turns a profit. A top executive who has rung up five consecutive quarters of massive growth has little incentive to do anything different except ask for a whopping raise.

Nonetheless, these firms may be the ones most vulnerable to change by others. Complacency often precludes future success. We can all remember the secure executives at General Motors who didn't introduce small economy cars, or those at IBM who ignored the potential of the personal computer. While surely aware of major changes in their fields, top executives of these firms might have felt much as Carlisle did in *Richard II* when he said, "Prevent it, resist it, let it not be so."

Both companies suffered gravely as their top leaders—who lost their jobs—forgot the Golden Rule of change in the business world: Do unto others before they do unto you.

The Encyclopaedia Britannica saw its sales of printed Encyclopaedia decline between 1990 and 1997. The culprit was a competitive CD-ROM reference library that could be dropped into a pocket. Today, Britannica has its own CD-ROM encyclopedia at a cost that is about 10 percent of the price of its hardbound version.

Levi Strauss is another example of a well-established company in which executives failed to challenge themselves to force change in recent years. In 1998, Levi's sales dipped 13 percent to $6 billion. Part of its problems stemmed from designer competitors like Tommy Hilfiger and less expensive labels offered at department stores like Sears. Because its sales were high in the early nineties, Levi Strauss & Co. didn't put enough thought into coming up with new styles.

Even the company's advertising focuses on the past. A recent campaign featured Marilyn Monroe sporting vintage jeans and a tag line that read, "Our models can beat up their models." Industry observers say Levi Strauss can recover—but it has to move forward with new styles that will attract teenage consumers.

Petruchio, on the other hand, both reacts to and instigates fundamental change, even though he really has no need to leave Verona. Then, in Padua, he undertakes the Herculean effort of remaking Katherine, although he could have settled for an easier task, or a simple future. He aims as high as he can.

John H. Costello, president of AutoNation, Inc., had little need to change his company, which had already grown into the largest auto dealership group in the United States. Its 223-unit car dealership chain in a traditional retail operation yielded $16.1 billion in sales in 1998, a 56.4 percent increase over 1997.

Nonetheless, Costello forced change. He had tried Internet marketing in his former position as senior executive vice president of marketing at Sears, Roebuck and wanted to do the same at AutoNation. Despite resistance to his plan, in 1998, he set up a test by having AutoNation create a Web site in Denver to promote local dealerships.

As it turned out, half the customers who visited AutoNation's stores that year said they wouldn't have done so without seeing its Web site. Thirty-five percent stated they would not have bought from the company if it hadn't advertised on the Internet. Costello also found that use of the Denver Web site tripled the size of a dealership's sales territory, drawing shoppers from a thirty-mile radius, as opposed to the traditional ten-mile range.

Sales leads from the Web resulted in $150 million in additional revenue for AutoNation during the first quarter of 1999. As a result, the company plans to create a similar national campaign.

The top management team must overrule change resisters in situations like Costello faced at AutoNation. These resisters become most vocal during times of mergers and acquisitions, when they claim that the ensuing change will not align with the "corporate culture."

Today's executives should answer such a charge the same way King Henry answered another Shakesperean Katherine's pleas about her own corporate culture during the time they discussed a merger (or, more accurately, an acquisition).

After conquering France, Henry wishes to marry Katherine, the princess of France. He tries to kiss her. She's aghast, saying in French that it is "not a fashion for the maids in France to kiss before they are married."

Henry simply sloughs off the objection by pointing out, "O Kate, nice customs curtsy to great kings." He goes on humorously but quite rightly, telling her, "Dear Kate, you and I cannot be confined within the weak list of a country's fashion. We are the makers of manners, Kate, and the liberty that follows our places stops the mouth of all find-faults."

Today's executives who hear Katherine-like protests against change must answer them. Speaking like Henry or acting like Petruchio, who breaks cultural conventions during Bianca's wedding feast, can make the point that cultural mores and traditions are the antithesis of change. They are rooted in the past, whereas change is pointed at the future.

Still, many elements of a corporate culture are invaluable, especially a firm's commitment to ethical operation, quality products, and respect for fellow employees. Corporate culture can also be a powerful force to help bind people together, indicate what is expected of them, and encourage them to learn from one another.

Too many "fault-finders" or change resisters nonetheless use the concept of corporate culture more as an excuse than an asset. Before General Electric Aerospace and Martin Marietta joined together in 1993, management teams of both companies were besieged with complaints that the two corporate cultures differed fundamentally. This became evident when employees from the two companies who worked in the same discipline held an initial videoconference to become acquainted. Martin Marietta employees showed up in business suits while the GE contingent wore sport shirts and slacks.

A week later the second videoconference opened to a burst of laughter. There, on the large TV screen, were suit-wearing GE employees, while those from Martin Marietta had dressed casually.

The merging of the companies lent itself to a consolidation of cultures as well. In fact, this melding of cultures and picking the best ideas and practices from each one proved to be the basis for an expanded organization that, after a series of mergers, now produces more than $26 billion in sales each year.

Other companies have also found that ignoring the naysayers can bring significant success. Just a few years ago, Radio Shack was having trouble getting manufacturers to ship their products to its increasingly outdated stores. The company hadn't done well since the eighties, when it sold personal computers priced as low as $300. Then, in 1996, Leonard Roberts, Radio Shack's chairman, president, and CEO who joined the company in 1993, launched a turnaround. He saw that electronics manufacturers were tired of selling their wares in huge superstores where the salespeople had little knowledge of their products. Now, Roberts thought, manufacturers might appreciate the high level of service Radio Shack's stores offered to customers.

Soon the company sold or shut down seventeen Incredible Universe superstores, which were originally intended to become the Ikea of consumer electronics. By 1998, Radio Shack also sold its ninety Computer City superstores to CompUSA. This left the management team free to concentrate on its nearly seven thousand Radio Shack stores.

In the meantime, though, when Roberts conveyed his plan to revive the Radio Shack stores, staffers laughed uproariously. His goal was to update the stores and have suppliers pay for it. This seemed very unrealistic. When Radio Shack decided to use IBM as its exclusive PC supplier in 1994, IBM had not agreed to contribute anything to refurbishing Radio Shack's stores. It seemed unlikely for IBM or any other supplier ever to do so.

Then opportunity arose. When Roberts discovered that Radio Shack's telephones were its most oft-purchased items and that women were most likely to buy them, he had stores focus on selling phones. As a result, one-third of the store's customers are now female, up from one in five the year he took his job.

Because of this emphasis on telephones, when Sprint needed retail space to sell its wireless services, its executives turned to Radio Shack. Furthermore, Sprint agreed to pump money into sprucing up the Radio Shack stores in 1996. Compaq, the computer manufacturer, struck a similar deal in 1998. Then, in April 1998, Radio Shack made a deal with Northpoint Communications Group to sell high-speed Web access from its stores.

The results of Roberts's once-snickered-at approach have been overwhelmingly positive for Radio Shack. Tandy, its parent company, like Gloucester in *Henry VI, Part II*, can feel that "the world may laugh again," since Radio Shack's sales for the first six months of 1999 totalled $1.75 billion, up from $1.5 billion the same period last year, amounting to a 16 percent increase.

LESSON FIVE

"Kiss the lips of unacquainted change."

—Cardinal Pandulph, in *King John*

An executive should implement change quickly and boldly, even when instincts and counsel dictate otherwise. Though the precise effects of the change may be unknown, the change itself should be embraced whole-heartedly.

Most employees within a company will argue for a slow and deliberate pace when implementing change. "Tut, I like it not," they may say to proposed change, much like Bianca in *The Taming of the Shrew.* "Old fashions please me best. I am not so nice to change true rules for odd inventions."

They resist rapid change for sound reasons, including feeling that the disruption will thereby be minimized, giving everyone more time to adjust, and spreading transition costs over more time. Such advice is logical, attractive, and generally wrong.

Most executives who adopt such moderation later believe it was mistaken. A recent survey shows that after mergers and acquisitions—a prospect hitting ten on the corporate Richter scale—nearly 90 percent of the managements involved wished they had introduced change faster. Only one in ten felt they should have moved more deliberately.

While many people initially resist change, most adjust soon enough. They not only want but deserve to know all the facts about what is going on. Then they generally confront the change head-on, get it over with, and move on with their professional and personal lives.

Most executives realize that more business mistakes stem from clinging to a good idea too long than from jumping to a new idea too early. Abandoning an idea before it has a chance to prove its worth is another common corporate error.

"The affair cries haste," Othello says, "and speed

must answer it." Certainly Petruchio works fast and is bold. He lets little time lapse in his taming of the shrew.

For, as Shakespeare knew, time has a way of fouling up a situation. As the Bard wrote in his Sonnet 115: "Reckoning Time, whose million accidents creep in 'twixt vows, and change decrees of kings, tan sacred beauty, blunt the sharpest intents, divert strong minds to the course of altering things."

One company that has reaped the benefits of embracing change quickly is Volkswagen. In 1993, the year Ferdinand Piëch, the grandson of engineer Ferdinand Porsche, took the helm of the automobile manufacturing company, VW lost $1.1 billion. Piëch, who had worked previously at Porsche and VW's Audi unit, was confident that he knew what it would take to raise profits. His simple turnaround strategy was to find ways to make high-quality, reasonably priced cars that consumers would love at less expense to the company. Still, even for a company known for its expertise in making affordable cars, achieving this goal wasn't easy, given the prevailing mood at the troubled firm.

Every time Piëch suggested something new, opposition seemed to come from all directions, from assembly-line union workers to top-level managers. When faced with such fervent opposition, Piëch did what Henry V advises in such a situation: "Gracious lord, stand for your own. Unwind your bloody flag."

He swiftly did what he felt needed to be done. To save money, he introduced a four-day workweek for some employees. This didn't exactly go over well in Germany, where unions have a strong presence, but he

kept his own bloodied flag unfurled. He also stream-
lined the company's twelve-man management team to a
leaner five people, even though giving the others the ax
created instant enemies.

In addition, to improve the company's image, he
took the risk of spending $1 billion to buy the Bentley,
Bugatti, and Lamborghini brands in 1998. Now he is
moving forward on a plan to use five basic prototypes
for all of the cars the company manufactures, which
should save the company money—as long as he keeps
quality high enough to attract consumers.

Thanks to Piëch's eagerness to move quickly, the
company's pretax profits rose to $3.6 billion last year.
According to surveys by J. D. Power & Associates, VW
has also boosted quality more than has any other car-
maker in the past five years.

LESSON SIX

"Nimble thought can jump both sea and land."

—Sonnet 44

Corporate plans should be kept broad enough to allow
for adjustments. While Petruchio sets an overall goal—
to find a wealthy wife in Padua—he keeps it broadly
scoped. He doesn't specify just what wife, how much
wealth, or what might constitute happiness. Nonetheless,
Petruchio finds Katherine, already endowed with the
same intelligence, rebelliousness, and wit that he has,
and molds her into a true partner.

Many of today's corporate staffs waste staggering

amounts of time, effort, and resources to specify every element of a strategic plan in minute detail. Companies spend months developing point-by-point strategies and financial projections for the next five years, while missing financial projections for the next quarter.

It is wiser to form a clear sense of the general goal, prepare for various contingencies, and then be poised for opportunities that happen along, or (better yet) are created.

Jim Amos, president and CEO of Mail Boxes, Etc., found that such flexibility pays off handsomely. When his company created a new Internet service provider to compete with America Online in 1997, his staff undertook a huge amount of planning. Prepared to invest $5 million in the project, the executives wished to pinpoint their target customers. They decided to go after those who worked outside of traditional offices in so-called nontraditional companies.

Eight months into the project, Amos realized that this approach was floundering. It proved harder than anticipated to reach "nontraditional" companies. About that time, Mail Boxes, Etc., merged with U.S. Office Products. Amos then decided to form partnerships, and in September 1998, Mail Boxes, Etc., launched a new type of service in conjunction with IBM and InfoSeek.

Called MBE Online, this Internet provider targeted people who used Mail Boxes, Etc., services daily. Under Amos's nimble leadership and this new approach, the firm thrives. The projected revenue for 1999 is $1.5 billion, up from $1 billion in 1998.

Like Amos, after selecting a broad overall goal, corporate executives should lay out plans to reach it—but flexibility is crucial. As Petruchio demonstrates nicely, this takes four steps:

First, select clearly definable actions. In his case, it is to be married to someone wealthy and then to mold her into a loving and sharing partner.

Second, specify who is responsible for each action, and establish a deadline. This is no problem for Petruchio, who is a one-man management team. His timetable for marriage is "Sunday next" and for taming of the shrew as soon as possible.

Third, define measurable milestones to test the plan's progress. After trying his first approach, Petruchio realizes there's nothing to measure since Kate hasn't improved. Later, on the road back to Padua, he establishes two milestones (calling the moon the sun and giving a kiss in public). After reaching both, Kate is ready to be tested back in her own villa in front of everyone.

Fourth, allow for contingencies. Petruchio's elaborate undertaking of reforming Katherine's character cannot be expected to proceed without a few hiccups along the way. Therefore, he formulates a backup scheme, which he uses with great success.

Laying out a plan for change can reap great benefits for any successful company and its leaders. Shakespeare captures this joy of success in yet another Katherine, this one the Queen in *Henry VIII*.

She describes the pleasure that Petruchio, Bill

Lederer, Robert Shaw, Fernando Espuelas and Jack Chen, Leslie Wexner, Prospero, John Costello, Leonard Roberts, Ferdinand Piëch, Jim Amos, and Henry V can feel from implementing change with success.

"I am happy," Queen Katherine says, for having conducted herself with openness and kindness, as if "my actions were tried by every tongue, every eye saw them, envy and base opinion set against 'em. I know my life so even." Her last lesson, too, is a good one: "Truth loves open dealing."

ACT III

MAKING YOUR PLAY IN BUSINESS

"Things Won Are Done.

Joy's Soul Lies in the Doing."

[DRAMATIS EXECUTIVUS SUMMARIUS]

Making plans is one thing. Making plans reality is quite another. How to turn intentions into results entails the nitty-gritty of business, whether in modern corporations or ancient Roman empires. As welcome as big profits always are, many of the pleasures of business lie in the day-to-day challenges of the work, as Cressida points up in the above quote from *Troilus and Cressida*.

In *Julius Caesar*, a play that is all business and little play, the main characters are "organization men" who posture much of the time and are acutely aware of their roles in the establishment.

Ambitious men who must build teams, they judge each other carefully. Leaders who strive to instill trust, they organize their teams and implement their plans under treacherous conditions. They constantly gauge public opinion and communicate their message with considerable spin and varying success. And, as they hold meetings and make decisions, they accept individual responsibility. "The fault, dear Brutus, is not in our stars but in ourselves," as Cassius says. They use their reasoning powers but fully appreciate how fate and luck heavily affect results. Responding to teammates and opponents alike, they worry over their place in the corporate structure, as well as their ultimate success.

Their concerns are real, for problems constantly arise. Most are addressed and some even redressed. And, as always in Shakespeare, failures are a big part of the package. Each character is torn by choices while coping with practical situations as best he can. Each one makes more than a few mistakes and suffers more than a few business reversals.

In short, these real-life characters work hard to succeed. From their experiences contemporary corporate leaders can find answers to that all-important question, "How can I get the job done?"

PROLOGUE

Rome is poised for a bull market of economic and imperialistic expansion as far as the forecasters can see. Consequently common citizens adore their maximum leader, Julius Caesar.

Yet some uncommon nobles, like Cassius, do not. It is not that he minds what Caesar *does*, since he succeeds at everything he takes on. Rather, it is what he *is*, which is great and haughty. Cassius, tough and shrewd on the outside, is fragile within. He complains that "Caesar doth bear me hard" and measures most people by how they treat him.

Cassius faces an even tougher challenge than do hard-pressed modern executives. His enterprise—to rid Rome of Julius Caesar—demands great speed, stealth, and certitude. Attaining 90 percent of the goal cannot be deemed mission success. One should never wound the king.

Cassius's skills are suited to organizing a conspiracy. He has boundless energy, cunning, and the type of courage Caesar himself admires when saying that "cowards die many times before their deaths; the valiant never taste of death but once." More of an entrepreneur than a corporate type, Cassius requires the assistance of specialists because this project is complex, and a wise manager recognizes when he cannot do the job alone.

Shakespeare scribed a dozen plays on "divine right" kings, virtually none of them godlike leaders. Here, however, he portrays a self-made man who made himself quasi-divine. Though he appears in only three scenes, utters only 150 lines, and dies in the middle of the play, Julius Caesar dominates the drama.

Caesar's accomplishments are staggering. He excels as a military strategist and tactician, extending Rome's rule across Europe right up to the shores of the Atlantic. Between stunning victories, he expands Rome's economy, codifies its laws, builds libraries, and promotes great architecture. Awesome, too, is the breadth of his personal talents, as his interests range across official, domestic, intellectual, and charitable activities.

His mind conquers even more than his armies. Shakespeare would have been impressed by Caesar's literary skills, especially the crisp and lively *Commentaries*. Once while crossing the Alps, he wrote a textbook on grammar and articles on astronomy and mathematics. During another segment of down time, he devised the calendar still in use today (the month of July is named in his honor).

In the play, Caesar's successes are acknowledged by his contemporaries. Every key character considers him "a dish fit for the gods" and most of the noble Romans think and operate largely in relation to him. Mark Antony calls him "the noblest man that ever lived in the tide of time." Even Cassius uses superlatives when describing Caesar, and Brutus calls him simply "the foremost man of all this world."

Yet, Shakespeare draws him as a real person. Cassius recalls Caesar's near drowning when they were swimming together. Caesar falls in an epileptic fit in the public square. While doing some management by walking around, he asks Antony to "come on my right hand, for this ear is deaf."

Physically imperfect, Caesar is also personally flawed. He proclaims himself fearless, yet his wife scares the daylights out of him when relating her nighttime dreams. He boasts of being as fixed as the northern star, yet he's skittish about going to work on the Ides of March (and with good reason). He claims to seek no higher office, yet he comes alive before a crowd. Ironically he seems less sure-footed in private than before the stockholders.

A flawed man but a man in full, Julius Caesar is now a man in danger.

Scene I

[Enter a shrouded fellow speaking to a nobleman whose paunch extends his toga]

At the top of the executive order, a lonely post where one must listen particularly carefully to avoid becoming isolated, Caesar commits the serious error of ignoring important information that comes his way. Both his wife and the soothsayer warn him of imminent danger. A staffer even drafts an internal memorandum on the growing conspiracy against him and pleads, "O Caesar, read mine first, for mine's a suit that touches Caesar nearer."

Caesar ignores their warnings. He is an overconfident, overworshipped leader with plenty of willing followers. Antony says, "When Caesar says 'Do this,' it is performed."

One indicator of his authority is the success of his subordinates. Good managers are good mentors who develop those around and beneath them. They create growth opportunities for subordinates, even if it means losing them to other offices in the organization. Caesar develops his staff, who in turn place him on a pedestal. In business, strong leaders build strong companies. The persona of the leader is reflected many times over—for better or worse. But the stronger the leader, the greater the problems likely to be encountered in any succession transition, which is a warning of things to come.

Caesar is aware of Cassius and his jealous ambitions. Among Caesar's finest executive talents is his ability to judge others. Early on Caesar confides to Antony: "Yon Cassius has a lean and hungry look. He thinks too much."

Caesar calls Cassius a cynic—"He looks quite through the deeds of men"—and knows Cassius lacks outside interests: "He loves no plays. He hears no music." Also, he has a major attitude problem: "Seldom he smiles, and smiles in such a sort as if he mocked himself and scorned his spirit." Likewise, corporate boards and managers should favor people committed to outside interests as well as their work. To insist on single-minded devotion to the firm is to accumulate personnel prone to lose perspective and eventually burn out.

Finally Caesar understands Cassius's biggest flaw. "Such men as [Cassius] be never at heart's ease whiles they behold a greater than themselves," he says with blazing insight. "And therefore are they very dangerous."

Caesar is right. Treacherous Cassius is now looking for support from esteemed nobles because his squad lacks heavy hitters, or the crucial 10 percent of the contributors who, in any pursuit, account for 30 percent of the results. Whether in politics, sports, business, nonprofits, or, in Cassius's case, treachery, generally one-tenth of the team produces more than one-third of output. Once such big producers are aboard, enlarging the roster merely lowers the average output. However, Cassius is no insecure executive who surrounds himself with second-rate talent for fear of being upstaged . . . a not uncommon weakness of some modern managers who thus doom themselves to failure.

In a nutshell, Cassius needs Brutus, who is, and tells everyone he is, a paragon of virtue. Cassius opens his recruitment drive not with a fat incentive package but with personal schmoozing and tells Brutus that he feels from him less "gentleness and show of love as I was wont to have." This is not surprising, for Brutus is a Stoic, who loves principles, not people. He hates tyranny, though not the tyrant. A man easy to admire from afar, Brutus is insufferable to work with because he has no tolerance for human contradictions or weaknesses. Anyone this inflexible spells trouble in any organization, old or new.

Cassius, on the other hand, possesses the critical executive skill of understanding the needs of others. Appreciating that Brutus is a high-maintenance type, Cassius strains to provide him the strokes and attention he needs. Cassius endorses individual responsibility, telling him, "Men at some time are masters of their fates."

He suggests that they need not remain underlings to Caesar and he poses the cutting question. Why is "he . . . grown so great," he asks Brutus, and not *you?*

The two nobles receive a news flash from Casca. Caesar has been offered the crown three times and thrice refused it, each time less reluctantly. Brutus, always a heavy thinker, begins to stew over this development.

After they agree to meet again, Cassius cleverly

remarks to Brutus: "Till then, think of the world." An able executive, he keeps his principal objective in mind—here, recruiting Brutus—and does what it takes to achieve it.

Using the indirect approach as well, Cassius salts the Roman version of a corporate chat room with his own ideas. He flings supposedly anonymous letters from citizens concerned over "Caesar's ambitions" through Brutus's windows, informing him of the conspiracy to be rid of Caesar. This phony "citizens' drive" appeals to Brutus's patriotism. In his mind, nothing Caesar *does* warrants his demise, but there is always what he *might* do. Then Brutus ponders a phenomenon common in business and politics: those, like Caesar, who may forget ex-colleagues once they make it to the top. This forget- fulness is as big a mistake in business as it is in politics, since no one stays at the top forever. Furthermore, neglected colleagues may even hurry a premature retire- ment ceremony along.

Meanwhile Cassius keeps his teammates informed, as good managers do. He tells them that he is working hard on the Brutus matter, and that it is going well. While Brutus broods, Cassius and his conspirators cir- cle in for the deal-closer. As in any sensitive business transaction, especially a merger, participants fear leaks. It seems almost a trick of the Roman gods that corpora- tions have such difficulty getting publicity on positive developments but receive in-depth coverage when an unwanted leak occurs.

As Cassius realizes, keeping secret matters secret cannot be taken for granted. Interestingly most business leaks do not spring from a participant beeping a journalist or competitor, although there are a few would-be Paul Reveres around. Even fewer are due to flagrant carelessness. Rather, most come from clues. Good companies hire observant people, and they are fully capable of detecting and interpreting signs that something is afoot. Such people quickly notice a new behavior pattern such as numerous closed-door meetings of the firm's top officers or sudden repeated trips to a particular city.

The conspirators teach us six steps today's executives should use to help maintain secrecy. First, Cassius keeps his team small. Second, its members continue their normal routines as best they can. Third, they act with dispatch, so as to reduce exposure time. In fact, Cassius's conspirators intend to meet, greet, and defeat Caesar the very next morning.

Fourth, they draw up a list of those who need to know and ensure that everyone named knows precisely who else is on the list—and, more important, who is *not* on it. Fifth, they introduce "noise" into the system to confuse anyone stumbling onto the secret information or suspecting something is up. The more rumors ricocheting around, the harder it is for an outsider to tell which one is true.

Sixth, they draw up a pledge of secrecy. Cassius suggests they "swear our resolution" in a formal oath. In really important matters, today's executives should have their corporate lawyers draft a document certifying that all signatories pledge to maintain secrecy. This entails not discussing the matter with anyone other than those in the know, and, most important, taking actions that preclude tipping off observant outsiders. Having the corporation's general counsel perform a formal though private "signing ceremony" helps convey the seriousness of that pledge.

Here no one questions the gravity. Yet there is no pledge, since Brutus opposes Cassius's suggestion to enact one. While perhaps wrong in a situation of such extreme sensitivity, Brutus makes the sound point for modern managers that trust is the best glue to bind together the members of a team. Management reaps greater success when clearly trusting team members to do their jobs, and do them well, rather than suspecting otherwise. But this does not imply that a manager need not remind the members of the team what is expected of them.

Cassius makes yet another sound suggestion. "But what of Cicero?" he asks gently, sensing that one more noble Roman icon may be one too many for Brutus. "I think he will stand very strong with us." Cassius's instincts are right, for standing next to the upstanding Cicero in public would be the ancient equivalent of a photo op.

Everyone agrees except Brutus, but that's enough to nix the notion. Brutus, unlike Cassius, commits the unpardonable management sin of excluding the best talent to do the job for fear of being overshadowed.

"O name him not." Brutus rejects the idea from Cassius by claiming that Cicero always rejects ideas not invented here. According to Brutus, Cicero will "never follow anything that other men begin." This moment marks a milestone for this management structure, the first major mistake due to Brutus's shortage of judgment and abundance of arrogance. Once Cassius recruits Brutus, he effectively hands over management control. As he puts it: "Brutus shall lead, and we will grace his heels."

So begins an organizational behavior pattern that eventually destroys the management team. Time and again Cassius proposes a shrewd action, Brutus objects, and Cassius caves. Brutus is so wrapped in his own obtuse notions that he is capable of rendering any organization dysfunctional, and Cassius commits that greatest of all business disloyalties. He does not tell the emperor, or in this case Brutus, that he is without a toga.

Nonetheless Caesar's ruin looms near. Having recruited Brutus, Cassius and his clique are pumped as they head toward the Capitol for their final dealing with Caesar.

Scene II

[Enter a group of men wearing sandals and long togas, hooded to hide their faces]

Once assembled, the conspirators create "noise" by approaching Caesar with a plea to pardon Publius Cimber, whom Caesar has banished.

In response, Caesar pontificates on the virtues of order and constancy: "I do know but one that unassailable holds on his rank, unshaked of motion. . . . And that I am he."

While Julius Caesar extols stability and order, chaos

is unleashed as the conspirators strike. No executive is more vulnerable than when busy admiring himself. As Caesar falters from repeated stabs, the conspirators spin their message by shouting "Liberty! Freedom! Tyranny is dead!" and "Liberty, freedom, and enfranchisement!"

Finally, about to die, the great man utters, *"Et tu, Brute!*—Then fall, Caesar!"

Brutus then seeks to raise the deed from murder to a ritual offering. He asks his comrades to "Stoop, Romans, stoop, and let us bathe our hands in Caesar's blood up to the elbows." As their hands drip red, Antony enters this macabre scene. Initially traumatized, he swiftly pulls himself together. Keeping his reason, he can also see that he is vastly outnumbered and distinctly unwanted. While Antony can't avenge Caesar's murder just then, he can make the best of a very bad situation. Thus begins the rise of Antony and the fall of Brutus and company.

Brutus scampers to explain, "O Antony, beg not your death of us, though now we must appear bloody and cruel." Brutus promises he'll soon stand in front of the shareholders and tell "why I, that did love Caesar when I struck him," participated in the murder.

Antony feigns accommodation, stating, "I doubt not of your wisdom," and then systematically begins to ruin the conspirators. He says simply, "Let each man render me his bloody hand" and moves around the stage to greet each person like a toga-wearing maître d'.

Antony's hand-shaking is a brilliant stroke of team-wrecking. His one-on-one maneuver individualizes each assassin. Mob psychology may have prevailed before and during the deed, but individual responsibility follows it, as it always must.

After circling the group, Antony asks for time to share his thoughts at Caesar's funeral, and Brutus unwisely grants it. Cassius, comporting himself as COO rather than a full partner, privately questions Brutus's decision. Being direct with a manager is best, but Cassius is a bit too candid, telling him, "You know not what you do," and explains his position: "Know you how much the people may be moved by that which he will utter?" When a top manager must worry about who will be allowed to make a presentation to the board or a shareholder's meeting, that manager's days are numbered. Still, the planning proceeds. Brutus will speak first at the funeral and tell the citizens that Antony speaks only by their consent. Hence "it shall advantage more than do us wrong."

Cassius doubts that, but he again accedes to Brutus's decision.

By now, Cassius should be wondering about his CEO's judgment. Anyone in business who ends up with a leader like Brutus should move on as quickly as possible or risk sinking along with him.

Just how fast becomes clear when Brutus and Antony eulogize Caesar. In one of history's most celebrated funerals, their verbal face-off demonstrates communications approaches that contrast in both style and effectiveness. Each of them, like good executives before any important public appearance, is prepared. Both are convincing. Yet their differences are greater than their similarities. Brutus speaks prose and appeals to the head; Antony speaks poetry and appeals to the heart. Brutus uses concepts; Antony uses props, including Caesar's mutilated body and his will. Brutus's speech seems written out and read from a text; Antony's seems spontaneous and responsive to the audience's feelings. Brutus calls for reason; Antony calls for rebellion.

Brutus initially faces a skeptical audience as the citizens scream: "Let us be satisfied!" He explains that he "rose against Caesar . . . not [because] I loved Caesar less, but that I loved Rome more." Had Caesar lived, he warns, they might all have ended up as slaves.

As Antony approaches Caesar's body, Brutus introduces him by saying that "though [Antony] had no hand in his death," he will "receive the benefit of his dying." The speech is well received but not well understood. Though Brutus warned against Caesar's tyranny, the citizens react by shouting, "Let him be Caesar." Mum, Brutus doesn't resist this succession planning by the citizenry since they want *him* to be the successor.

While Brutus surely prepared his concepts, Antony prepared for his audience. In our era of global communications, executives cannot deliver different messages to various audiences. The union, shareholders, media, politicians, and mid-managers must all hear the same basic message. While being consistent, however, the emphasis can be fitted to the interests of the particular audience. Employees are keenest to hear how new developments affect jobs, benefits, and work demands. Stockholders like to hear about shareholder return; rating agencies are interested in leverage, coverage, and the like.

Should the executive fail to mold the message to the listening audience, that audience won't be listening for long. This outcome can be prevented by applying what Antony must have considered: If I were in the listener's sandals, what would I want to learn?

Antony avoids three common errors of contemporary corporate communications. First, he shies away from expending so much effort on perfecting the contents that no time is left to prepare its delivery. Business plans and actions can be carefully crafted, but when the presentation of well-crafted executive words is tossed together at the last moment, that carelessness inevitably shows.

Second, Antony does not allow anyone else to control his message. When appearing before the press, especially on television, some executives feel compelled to stick to the media's script. They should, instead, stick to their own script—regardless of the questions asked. And they should know what message the script must convey.

Antony speaks under Brutus's tight conditions, including avoiding any blame of the conspirators, but he doesn't lose his own focus. He may adhere to the letter of the conditions imposed but not to the spirit of those conditions.

Third, Antony shuns the common temptation to deliver a plethora of messages. The higher an executive's position, the fewer the messages that can be effectively conveyed. Top executives have too little contact time with particular stockholders, employees, suppliers, analysts, or community leaders to risk imparting too many important messages at once. Some CEOs choose to boil down their presentation to three thrusts: (1) operate ethically, (2) provide quality products and services, and (3) be people oriented and support the team. When these things are done, profits take care of themselves. Besides, no worker was ever inspired by emotional speeches on profits.

Antony heads for the pulpit with his message condensed to these same three points: (1) the conspirators did not operate ethically, (2) Caesar provided quality products and services to the populace, and (3) the populace should support his—Antony's—team.

With the crowd still abuzz with praise for Brutus, Antony delivers the classic public communication opening, "Friends, Romans, countrymen, lend me your ears!"

First, Antony echoes Brutus' nice rhythms: "I come to bury Caesar, not to praise him. The evil that men do lives after them, the good is oft interred with their bones. So let it be with Caesar."

But then he turns from melodic to mocking. "Brutus hath told you Caesar was ambitious. If it were so, it was a grievous fault, and grievously hath Caesar answered it. . . . For Brutus is an honorable man. So are they all, all honorable men."

He celebrates Caesar's service in ways the audience grasps. After each of Caesar's military victories, he brought back booty that he put in "the general coffers." He cared for the needy. He thrice refused the "kingly crown." Was this ambition?

After this polished opening, Antony gets personal. He asks the audience to "bear with me" since "my heart is in the coffin there with Caesar." He walks over to the corpse and breaks down. After heroically collecting himself, Antony says that he holds Caesar's will but won't read it. He tells them, "You are not wood. You are not stones, but men. And, being men, hearing the will of Caesar, it will inflame you, it will make you mad."

After playing the crowd a bit more, Antony gives in. First, however, he bids the public to encircle Caesar's mutilated corpse. "If you have tears, prepare to shed them now," he warns as he points out which stab was made by which conspirator (as if he knew).

This provokes members of the gathering to cry out, "Revenge! About! Seek! Burn! Fire! Kill! Slay! Let not a traitor live!"

The citizens begin to rampage when Antony reminds them, "You have forgot the will I told you of." As luck would have it, Caesar's will is most generous to these very citizens. It bestows upon them cash dividends, new walkways, trees, orchards—a veritable cornucopia of big government pork for Rome.

With that announcement, Caesar's funeral, support for the conspirators, and virtue and order for Rome are history. "Now let it work," Antony muses to himself, as his revolution gets launched. Cassius and Brutus, once on the march for liberty, go on the run for their lives. They must arm and fight. Now it is Antony's turn to get organized and build a team in his attempt to avenge the murder of Julius Caesar.

∽

SCENE III

[Enter three soldiers, who exchange cold looks and minimal greetings and then sit down to talk business.]

A savvy businessman, Antony seeks allies with hard assets. Octavius Caesar is smart and has the biggest and best military forces. As Caesar's grandnephew and adopted son, he also adds the Caesar mantle to the team. However, while he brings resources, he lacks appeal. Like many failure-prone executives, he wears his ambition on his sleeve. The careers of many capable managers implode once they became fixated on climbing up the corporate structure. Even after achieving early career success, they become so bitten by ambition that they concentrate on looking up the corporate ladder, rather than down directly at their jobs. In contrast, managers who treat every job as if it were their last will have superiors standing in line to get them on the next rung of *their* ladder.

The third leg in the new triumvirate is Lepidus. He, too, has troops, but little else.

While the opposition has already adopted a traditional hierarchical corporate structure, these three fall into an entrepreneurial, nonorganization structure of equals. Like many Silicon Valley startups, they shun titles or clear lines of authority. All initially seem interchangeable and will—like so many others—work together for a time, achieve fast success, and then split apart to compete with one another.

Meanwhile they must make that quick hit. Consequently they work fast. Tradition-bound managers set their schedules to the clock, presumably figuring that because the day is divided into hours, they should schedule a meeting for each one. But executives are far more efficient dividing their office time into ten-minute segments, and allocating them according to the importance and complexity of the issue to be addressed. Scheduling a regular morning meeting for information exchange in an area without chairs invariably eliminates irrelevant conversations and cuts meeting time to one or two segments.

These three Romans conduct their well-run business in one brief, substantive, and direct meeting. Questions are asked and answered crisply. Possible objections are raised openly and addressed frankly. Decisions are made, notes taken, and follow-up actions assigned. Deadlines are set and results monitored.

Everything is ideal in Shakespeare's model of a well-run business meeting except its agenda. The three are there to refine a death list.

Someone has presumably distributed a parchment agenda ahead of time, since all three come prepared. Antony opens the meeting and gets to the point: "These many then shall die, their names are pricked." Octavius openly raises a potential conflict of interest: "Your brother too must die," he tells Lepidus, and bluntly asks if he's on board. "Consent you, Lepidus?" When told "I do consent," Octavius instructs the note-taker: "Prick him down, Antony."

Then Lepidus turns prickly. "Publius shall not live," he says and reminds them that he's "your sister's son,

Mark Antony." Eyes then turn to Antony, who says he's on board with that. "He shall not live. Look, with a spot I damn him." Antony assigns responsibility for follow-up: "Lepidus, go you to Caesar's house . . . and we shall determine how to cut off" the opposition. As Lepidus undertakes his errand, Antony bad-mouths him to Octavius, calling Lepidus "a slight, unmeritable man, meet to be sent on errands." In short, Lepidus receives a poor performance review. Here perhaps demonstrating poor management practices, Antony fails to discuss the performance review with the one person who might be able to do something about it: Lepidus. On the other hand, perhaps Anthony treats Lepidus like a contingency worker, his chops needed only for a particular project and thus not worth developing for long-term employment.

Supervisors today sometimes encounter employees who resemble Lepidus. They're not untrustworthy but they are only minimally competent. Lepidus "must be taught, and trained, and bid go forth," Antony says. But Lepidus is later shoved aside and given an ancient version of two-weeks notice by Octavius.

While this three-sided team is all cold business, the Cassius-Brutus team is all hot passion as they journey off to participate in that much-maligned institution, a company off-site gathering. Considered to be assemblages of earth-shattering importance to the invited, and gross boondoggles to the uninvited (and media), corporate off-sites can, in fact, prove powerful tools. They permit far more uninterrupted discussion and undiluted team-building than possible in meetings back at the office, especially if substantial periods are left open for informal discussion between scheduled sessions.

The Team Brutus off-site, however, is no model of team-building. Instead, it is Shakespeare's superb example of an intense relationship undergoing a severe crisis. The Bard offers us perceptive insights into conflict escalation, resolution, and eventual yet incomplete reconciliation.

Cassius arrives all fired up, promptly accusing Brutus, "Most noble brother, you have done me wrong!" Brutus feigns ignorance and eggs him on by asking why. Cassius screams loud enough for Brutus to need to quiet him down, since their staff is hanging around. Emotional disagreements among senior executives cannot be tolerated—and certainly not in public. Otherwise, everyone chooses sides, and there is no longer a team.

Wisely Brutus suggests they retire to his tent. An officer is asked to clear the area and, in essence, put a DO NOT DISTURB sign on the flap. Once inside, the dispute grows still hotter. "Brutus, bait not me, I'll not endure it." Cassius stutters, "I am a soldier, I, older in practice, abler than yourself."

Brutus accuses Cassius of having an "itchy palm" and tolerating associates who take bribes. Cassius makes the profound point that, "a friend should bear his friend's infirmities" or faults. Yet, because he wears his virtue on his sleeve, "Brutus makes mine greater than they are." Cassius becomes so emotionally spent that he asks Brutus to kill him.

This has clearly gone beyond your classic watercooler disagreement. Even Brutus realizes that the con-versation has turned critical, and the Stoic apologizes. Healing is furthered when Brutus shares the shocking news that his dear wife, Portia, is dead. This sad revela-tion makes Cassius feel even worse. He cannot fathom how Brutus could have withheld such terrible informa-tion so long and seem so stoical about it.

They return to business and, as happens frequently in modern corporate life, they are bombarded with con-flicting information. One officer reports that Antony's team has "put to death an hundred senators," but Brutus claims that he has better information, that the true number is seventy. Like many corporate debates, the intensity of the argument is inversely proportional to the difference the options make.

Regardless, the news reinforces the high stakes of their partnership. If Antony's triumvirate slaughtered several dozen senators, including the esteemed Cicero, imagine what they might do to Cassius and Brutus. This information constitutes a veritable wake-up call to return to military matters. Brutus tries to flatter Cassius by asking the professional soldier's judgment, but stays true to form. He hears Cassius, but then abruptly over-rules him. "Good reasons must of force give place to bet-ter," he reminds him archly. Cassius concedes to him for the last time. This is their final decision together, and, like the others, it is a disastrous one. It marks the end of whatever job security either may have had.

Finally, the four leaders—Antony and Octavius, and Brutus and Cassius—meet on the battlefield. Octavius provides a model for any executive engaged in an intense internal dispute. When debates break out in corporate offices, as they invariably will in any active business stretching itself to achieve its goals, the team leader should take a cue from Octavius and break in with, "Come, come, the cause." Refocusing the discussion on what the team is attempting to achieve helps reunite its members. If the members can't agree on this, they have a still more serious problem to tackle. This rule is demonstrated here.

While Octavius and Antony like each other less than Brutus and Cassius like each other, they hang together for the moment because it is expedient.

Moreover, Octavius and Anthony are not so engrossed in their own relationship as to ignore the competition. The best team leaders—whether generals, CEOs, managers, or salespeople—know their competitors' tactics, products, strengths, and vulnerabilities virtually as well as they know their own. Shrewd companies even set up teams to study their competitors and strive to think like they do, thereby gaining a lead on their adversaries' next move. Above all, they never become ignorant or disdainful of their competitors, as Brutus does.

The denouement seems almost anticlimatic. The series of bad executive decisions, a rough relationship at the top, and the lack of focus on the competition have doomed Brutus and Cassius. Their luck has run out, and fate has turned against them. The battlefield becomes engulfed in the fog of war. Brutus makes a stupid tactical decision, even though his forces are actually winning. Cassius receives misinformation and, wrongly believing that his friend has been killed and all is lost, kills himself.

His dying breath speaks of the great man, "Caesar, thou art revenged, even with the sword that killed thee."

Brutus executes another attack, fails, abandons all hope, and asks his soldiers to kill him. No one will follow his orders. Hence Brutus dies on his own sword, much as he lived, by himself, saying, "Caesar, now be still. I killed not thee with half so good a will."

The triumvirate triumphs, but tenuously. Still more is fated to fall apart. Everything in the winner's camp, indeed everything in Rome, remains in turmoil—except the looming spirit of Julius Caesar: That is now as "constant as the northern star."

ACTING LESSONS

For a twenty-first-century executive, as for the ancient Romans, it's good business to set goals and turn them into reality. As *Julius Caesar* illustrates, the elements of getting the job done—once a plan is in place—include building and managing a team, succession planning, organizing the team, communicating the message, and implementing the plans.

LESSON ONE

"They well deserve to have that know
the strongest and surest way to get."

—King Richard II

As their first operating priority, corporate boards and executives must hire those who know the "strongest and surest way to get" where the company should go. What distinguishes a winner from a loser is disproportionately the business's board and top executives and how each functions while carrying out its respective responsibilities. Thus, ironically, a corporation's greatest assets appear nowhere on its balance sheet.

To maximize these assets, corporate personnel managers must locate, obtain, train, and retain the best talent possible to fill out the cast. Patty DeDominic, president and CEO of PDQ Personnel Services in Los Angeles, a company with $15.2 million in annual sales in 1998, has managed to attract talented employees by casting a wide net. She looks for able retirees by sending notices of job openings to the American Association of Retired Persons and the National Council on Aging. Her team joins advisory boards of local universities and community colleges which, in addition to affording worthwhile community service, provides opportunities to meet students who might make good temps. And she seeks out downsized executives at speeches she and her team give to business groups on career management: "Being where people are interested in developing their skills gives us constant contacts," she says. There people realize that "'tis the mind that makes the body rich," as Petruchio says in *The Taming of the Shrew.*

When it comes to the difficult task of predicting who will be the best choice from among several candidates, Shakespeare and most modern corporate executives agree: past performance is the single best indicator of future performance. Whether the candidate has left "monuments," that is, major accomplishments, is singularly revealing.

If there have been no past monuments, there probably won't be any future ones. On the other hand, a person with big achievements should rise fast. As Ventidius says in *Antony and Cleopatra:* "Who does in the wars more than his captain can, becomes the captain's captain."

To help increase the odds of recruiting success, whatever the level, a corporate board, executive, manager, supervisor, or headhunter should look for at least these traits:

1. *Personal attributes,* whether the person is of decent character, well-balanced, and has a life outside of work. While foremost, these personal attributes are not conclusive. Cassius, in fact, doesn't weigh other factors enough when he recruits Brutus solely on the basis of his virtue. Brutus's other traits, including being a loner, being afraid of others outshining him, not listening to others, and having poor judgment, prove fatal to his cause.

In an economy in which high-tech firms like Yahoo and Netscape can offer compensation packages that potentially rival those offered by long-established firms such as Andersen Consulting and Goldman Sachs, what makes one employer more attractive than another is often the corporate culture, that is, the work environment, and this is disproportionately determined by the CEO's personality. Few things are more motivating to employees than working for someone they genuinely like and respect—and few things are less motivational than working for someone who is not taken seriously.

Herb Kelleher's popularity is a big factor in the success of Southwest Airlines. His personality prompts flight attendants occasionally to entertain passengers with practical jokes, in addition to the more routine duties they perform. This motivates the employees and makes their sometimes repetitive jobs more fun. "The labor we delight in physics [heals] pain," as Macbeth pointed out.

Bishop Partners, an executive search firm in New York City, invested in creating a system by which employees could have access to the firm's computer network from home, twenty-four hours a day. The reason: It's tough for smaller firms to compete with bigger rivals when it comes to things like salary and traditional benefits.

With more two-career families trying to balance work and family, it's important to potential recruits to join a company where executives can not only have a rewarding career but can also have a life outside of work. Senior partners at Bishop, as well as employees who do research and consulting, are given the option of working from home two days a week. Many employees are young, have children, and live outside of Manhattan. "This is easier," says CEO Susan Bishop. Larger firms are now offering these benefits as well. For years, AT&T has, not surprisingly, been a leader in allowing its workers to telecommute.

Enron Corp., the Houston-based energy company, hires talented MBAs from top schools, then gives them rein to "make a body of a limb," as Aumerle states in *Richard II,* or create a niche in the company and turn it into a profit-making enterprise. "We stick them in the organization and tell them to figure something out," says president Jeffrey K. Skilling. As a result of this policy, the company has been able to build power plants and pipelines in Asia, Europe, and Latin America, in addition to the U.S., trade natural gas and electricity in wholesale markets, and create hedging instruments for the energy industry and commodities traders. Its stock price has rocketed upward, with the return on its shares reaching 972 percent between 1988, just before it instituted its free-spirited management approach, and 1999. The company recently reached a market capitalization of nearly $30 billion.

2. *Job skills,* or basic talent and knowledge. While indispensable, these are the easiest traits to find and identify. Knowledge of the primary skills of the job, like accounting, law, or engineering, are key attributes for those being considered for entry or mid-level positions. However, having these qualifications becomes increasingly commonplace when moving up the corporate ladder because of the personnel filtering process at each level. And, while outstanding people skills become pivotal for leaders in top positions, it is still important that they retain at least a basic understanding of the demands of lower-level jobs if they are to earn the respect of their teams. Nothing is more disheartening to employees than following orders from someone who hasn't bothered to learn company or industry basics.

3. *Motivation,* the inherent drive to stretch beyond what is expected or even thought possible. Motivation trumps talent every time. Steven R. Covey's 1989 book, *The 7 Habits of Highly Effective People,* would not have made it onto the business bestseller lists every year since he published it if this principle weren't so important. Hundreds of companies still train employees in the Covey system of prioritizing goals and focusing on

achieving them. *Time* named him one of the twenty-five most influential Americans of 1996 and put him on its cover. Interestingly Covey didn't come from the business world. When he started the first Covey Leadership Center in 1984, he was a little-known college professor who quit his job teaching at Harvard Business School to be able to apply his ideas.

4. *Teamwork,* or the ability to cooperate with others and suppress personal interests for the good of the common pursuit. Those who create conflict among colleagues or subordinates cannot be of benefit to today's corporation, where nearly all projects are team projects. The Brutuses in business suits who are too obstinate, or who refuse to heed others, cannot work any more effectively in business today than Brutus did in ancient Rome.

Basic loyalty is also a key ingredient of successful teamwork. The Computer Security Institute of San Francisco found, recently, that most security professionals had to deal with employees who obtained unauthorized access to their employers' computer systems. Many such breaches included the theft of proprietary information. Coupled with losses to outsiders who had broken into computer systems, these incidents cost each of the 124 companies surveyed an estimated $1 million in losses.

Besides looking for the positive traits noted so far, boards and top executives who are recruiting should watch for certain flashing lights warning of problems ahead. These include:

- The vertical pronoun, by which a candidate personalizes what was obviously a team success. Although Caesar boasts of his triumphs, he does acknowledge the role of others. A foolish job candidate today might mention how "I raised market share by twelve points," or "I had to reduce costs by thirty percent" when these were obviously "we" successes.

- Disrespect of or disdain for former bosses, colleagues, and especially competitors. Anyone spending fifteen minutes with Cassius would have heard him disparage his boss and colleagues. His organizing a personnel change at the top should not have come as much of a surprise.

- Job churning, where the candidate has frequently switched from company to company.

- Lengthy sabbaticals, where the candidate has been unemployed and apparently at leisure for an unduly long time. "If all the year were playing holidays," Hal says in *Henry IV, Part I*, "to sport would be as tedious as to work."

- Avoiding the kitchen, where the person has invariably held "assistant-to," "consultant," or "advisor" titles. Such positions usually entail little measurable performance or accountability. Holding a whole series of them may show an inclination to remain distant from the hazards of real responsibility.

- Too many constraints, where the candidate places inordinate emphasis on job location, working at home, specific position, or especially, title.

- Unharnessed ambition, as when the interviewee focuses heavily not on the specific job being considered but on the one after that. In *As You Like It,* Orlando speaks of places "where none will sweat but for promotion," not for the mission or the work itself. This intense focus on moving ahead will, Orlando says, "choke their service up" and make them less effective, and eventually less desirable in the position being considered, as well as in future jobs. The best employees are those who would "fling away ambition," as Cardinal Wolsey advises in *Henry VIII.*

- Peripheral vision, evidenced by too much concern for pay and vacation times. These points are important, but should always come second to focusing on the task to be performed. Desirable employees concentrate on building a career, not just finding a job.

- Extravagant promises, or unrealistic claims about turning around projects or even the entire business.

- Red alert, superficial or even "slick" answers, which may indicate a lack of seriousness or commitment but, worse yet, also may flag ethical problems ahead. A strong indicator of this syndrome is when an executive must ask a subordinate *exactly* the right question in order to determine what is really going on.

Besides interviewing candidates for the job, checking references is the next most helpful step. However, phoning the references given by the candidate isn't of much use by itself. For one thing, the candidate's current employer may be delighted at the prospect of unloading a major problem. Besides, legal barriers now discourage a totally candid assessment.

Secondary references, those solicited from the applicant's own suggested references, turn out to be more instructive, especially if they include colleagues and subordinates. Peers usually know a candidate's performance best of anyone in the organization and are invariably the most insightful judges. After several such inquiries, each moving further from the references offered by the job seeker, a truer picture of the candidate tends to emerge. It is also important, however, to guard against mere gossip. Ask specific questions to find out how well the respondent knows your candidate, and include asking for some information you already know to see how well the answer matches. In all cases, a personal discussion will be far more valuable in soliciting candor than one conducted over the phone.

Assessing existing employees has much in common with judging new candidates, except that the familiarity level is much higher.

One dilemma of assessing personnel performance in our age of collaborative projects is the difficulty of pinpointing individual contributions. Occasionally management may get it wrong, as Parolles says in *All's Well That Ends Well,* "The merit of service is seldom attributed to the true and exact performer." The top corporate executive often receives far more credit than he or she deserves when things are heading upward, and far more blame than is warranted when the organization is spiraling downward.

Employees, like Lepidus, who chronically fall short should not be allowed to continue as they are. Instead, supervisors should discuss with them their unimpressive performance calmly, objectively, and privately, stressing that the issue is *not* with them as people but with their effectiveness as employees. If the problem is not rectified soon thereafter, they must be dismissed without procrastination. The signal is sent that management has the courage to rectify problems and that it won't "look the other way." The company and its other employees are then relieved of the load they've carried and can move forward. "Where the offense is," as Claudius says in *Hamlet,* "let the great axe fall." Not uncommonly, the employees who receive the pink slip are also relieved, knowing better than anyone that they aren't getting the job done and looking forward to a fresh start elsewhere.

Leopoldo Fernandez Pujals, the founder of TelePizza SA, one of the most successful growth ventures in Europe, understands the fundamentals of personnel assessment. His company has excelled in a highly competitive market because of Pujals's attention to details such as the individual performance of key staffers in his nearly six hundred takeout pizza outlets. For instance, he logs complaints that part-timers make against each manager to make sure they are managing their teams effectively. He even tracks which stores and telephone operators sell the most side orders of garlic bread! Now, *that's* attention to detail. His company's shares are up 990 percent since its IPO in November 1996, with sales of $285 million in 1998.

Gauging whether an employee can effectively supervise others or oversee a large organization is inherently difficult. Some people work better *under* supervision than *giving* it. Others let authority go to their heads, much as Isabella lamented in *Measure for Measure*: "Man, proud man, dressed in a little brief authority" becomes "most ignorant of what he's most assured" and "plays such fantastic tricks before high heaven as to make the angels weep."

In evaluating employees, many firms use rating systems based on a rigid numerical curve. A common mistake, this technique broadcasts to half of all team members that they are below average. This is not the message management should seek to convey since people generally act in ways that fulfill the expectations of others, especially top leaders.

Instead, management should aim to help every employee to feel and act "above average." The performance review should be more descriptive than numerical, and designed to point out strengths as well as areas of potential improvement. The goal should be to motivate—not demoralize.

LESSON TWO

"Nothing in his life became
him like the leaving it."

—Malcolm, in *Macbeth*

Top corporate executives should have in place a plan for succession of all senior personnel.

Neither Cassius nor Brutus do any succession planning when they plot to kill Caesar. Their lack of a clear replacement creates a void in Rome's top ranks and confusion throughout the realm, which Antony and Octavius exploit to their own advantage.

Consideration should be given to the type of experience and broadening each manager should receive in the years ahead. But actual job reassignments should be made only after a major business milestone has been achieved. Otherwise, corporate accountability evaporates and personal responsibility becomes blurry. Under these circumstances, like Antony's mob, everyone becomes responsible for everything and no one responsible for anything.

A list of at least three potential candidates ready to step into each critical position should be available in the event the incumbent goes elsewhere. If that assessment reveals a talent gap, the management needs to groom new candidates, mostly (but not entirely) from within the company.

Hewlett Packard, as but one example, understands the importance of succession planning. When Lewis Platt announced he was planning to leave the top position, the company quickly assembled a short list of candidates. (Reportedly there were at least four major contenders for the job.) Carlton S. Fiorina, at that time the president of Lucent Technologies' Global Service Provider Business, was named president and CEO in July 1999.

Unless several candidates are available, succession planning can fail. Earle M. Jorgensen figured he would simply pass on leadership of his steel-and-aluminum-distribution company, Earle M. Jorgensen Co., to his son John. But John died in 1990 when he was sixty-four. That left his father, then in his nineties, struggling to find someone to run the company. Although he was still active and energetic, Jorgensen finally sold the firm to Kelso & Co., and took a seat on its board.

Habitual hiring of top employees from outside the company indicates something amiss with the personnel system. Besides, it's a morale-buster for current employees, who can come to feel like Ulysses in *Troilus and Cressida* when he speaks of how "good deeds past . . . are devoured as fast as they are made, forgot as soon as done." Past contributions are forgotten since "to *have done* is to hang quite out of fashion, like a rusty nail." Some outside hiring can instill objectivity and infuse fresh approaches. But hiring an outsider to fill the CEO post, HP notwithstanding, should be considered a last resort.

Because the tenure of CEOs is short (just five or six years on average for major firms), a top priority of all directors on the business stage is to have in the wings several individuals who could move to the limelight. The final selection is one of the most important decisions that CEOs and boards of directors ever make.

Succession planning needs to be discreet. It should never become a public contest among a covey of worthy candidates. Destructive rumors fly: "The Emperor's court is like the house of fame [wherein] the palace [is] full of tongues, of eyes, and ears," as Aaron says in *Titus Andronicus*. Employees begin siding with whomever they bet on as the winner in this great corporate sweepstakes. Teamwork soon suffers and the executives passed over frequently take their talents elsewhere.

This ever-dicey problem of corporate succession is at its trickiest in a family-owned business. No management book or seminar lecture can delve more deeply into this relationship—or magnify it more largely—than the two *Henry IV* plays. Prince Hal is constantly chewed out by his father, King Henry IV, for gallivanting with Falstaff and his lowlife cohorts rather than tending to the family business of running England and taking over new countries. Hal knows he is frittering away the years but likes to believe he is broadening his "life experiences." Besides, he doesn't seek to be like his father, whom he considers distant and uninterested in anything but work . . . sort of a regal workaholic.

As succession nears, this strained relationship deteriorates. The lonely King—ill and overworked—sinks toward death. Hal is yet again summoned home to the castle, but this time he finds not a fist-shaking father but an apparently expired one.

When Hal suddenly spots the crown lying beside his father, he cannot resist trying it on for size. Just then the King awakens, which startles Hal. "I never thought to hear you speak again."

The dying King still musters a zinger: "Thy wish was father, Harry, to that thought. I stay too long by thee, I weary thee."

As in the worst of corporate succession struggles,

the King accuses his son of "so [hungering] for mine empty chair that thou wilt needs invest thee with my honors before thy hour be ripe." He's sorely disappointed, "O foolish youth!" and skeptical about the succession plan: "Thou seekest the greatness that will overwhelm thee."

Hence when all doubt is removed about the identity of a successor, Shakespeare shows that timing it badly can cause personal pain as well as institutional turmoil.

Brandon Dawson experienced such a situation. His stepfather, William Austin, owned Minneapolis-based Starkey Laboratories, a hearing-aid manufacturer with more than $300 million in sales. By the time he was twenty-five Dawson was Starkey's national sales director. He thought he would eventually become chief executive, but in 1991 his mother and Austin entered a bitter divorce. The stepfather and stepson soon found themselves arguing much as Claudius and Hamlet do, and finally split. "There wasn't a snowball's chance in hell of him ever running this company," Austin says, thus closing yet one more exercise in succession planning gone bad.

LESSON THREE

"Many a thousand actions, once afoot,
end in one purpose, and be all well."

—Bishop of Canterbury, in *Henry V*

Organizing the team to pull a "thousand actions" together has become even more critical as products and services become more complex and a company's competition stiffer. Any major project needs skills far beyond those any one person could possess.

Management must transform the team into far more than the sum of its parts by pulling the talents of individuals together to produce synergy. "As many arrows loosed several ways come to one mark, as many ways meet in one town, as many fresh streams meet in one salt sea, as many lines close in the dial's center," continues the Bishop, so must disparate parts of the corporation collaborate for success. Both Cassius and Antony recognized the need to build teams; their fault was not in their organization but in their choice of stars.

One of the best ways to pull employees together is for the top layers of management to set an example of what is expected. That means putting the work first and the ego last. And in this evaluation of executive talent, Brutus finished last, dead last.

Teamwork calls for breaking down a complex task, which initially appears overwhelming, into manageable parts. Then it entails assigning each person his or her own inputs, outputs, and schedule. Frequently the key to later success is early planning, and specifically, it often means organizing the fewest and simplest possible interfaces between tasks. The most serious problems arise at the interfaces between people working on the same project, companies supporting one another, and components in a technology-driven system.

Managing large teams necessitates encouraging feedback from all levels. Sometimes the best way to generate useful feedback is to allow for a degree of anonymity. Jone Panavas, vice president and co-founder of SoftChoice, a software developer based in Norwalk, Connecticut, and Toronto, Canada, set up a weekly online publication to keep in contact with her team of three hundred employees. On each page of *SINews*, employees can respond to the content if they choose. Although they can include their names, they don't have to, so Panavas can get the tell-it-like-it-is feedback she needs to achieve the company goals.

When problems arise anywhere in the team, they must be addressed in the forthright manner Richard II prescribes so well: "Then call" the people having the problem before the team manager, "to our presence, face to face and frowning brow to brow, ourselves will hear the accuser and the accused freely speak."

For management to build effective teamwork requires proper incentives. A company should systematically reward teamwork as well as individual accomplishment. The best system may feature a composite rating that *multiplies* the individual and team ratings in a way that precludes awards for team successes despite individual failures or vice versa. This type of system, however; also needs a "divorce" process, perhaps based on written documentation, so that no team feels saddled with a dysfunctional member.

Offering top pay isn't the only way to lure and retain top talent—although there are few examples where it has hurt. In most Shakespearean plays, people join a team because of common ambitions for power, resentment of those in power, or plain mutual affection. Only rarely is money a major factor. When it is, it usually signifies something is awry.

Modern companies often find stock options even more attractive than higher salaries, particularly to younger employees who don't yet have dependents and are willing to take a bet on the big bang. Stock options also make appealing recruiting bait, particularly for startups, like those headed by Macbeth, Richard II, and Claudius, that don't have much else to offer. Some employees take stock options so seriously that their distribution has become a bone of contention in workplace discrimination suits. In May 1999, eight female employees sued West Group, a publisher of legal textbooks and the Westlaw online service. They claimed that they were denied the opportunity to buy shares in the company that were offered to men in comparable positions and asked for $500 million in damages. The federal district court judge in Tampa, Florida, decided that the stock program should be considered part of the company's basic compensation package. This meant it fell under Title 7 of the 1964 Civil Rights Act, which bans discrimination based on race or gender. West Group has recently appealed the ruling.

Beyond financial rewards, however, are the intangibles, such as words of praise and appreciation by colleagues, especially supervisors. Everyone likes to hear that they are appreciated and, more important, to *know* that they are appreciated. This often is a greater motivator than anything else. As Hermione remarks in *The Winter's Tale:* "One good deed dying [unspoken] slaughters a thousand waiting upon that [one]. Our praises are our wages."

Then there is the matter of job title. Generous but

not extravagant use of elevated titles is a positive to the people who get them, opens doors outside the company, and does little damage to the balance sheet.

Businesses need a sound organizational structure with clearly identifiable paths for rising through the ranks. The best organization chart reflects the goals and tasks of the corporation, as well as the talents and weaknesses of those occupying the boxes. The key business units at any level should ideally be roughly equivalent in size—whether in terms of revenues or employees—to assure a balanced sharing of the burden. Virtually no one should be assigned a deputy, since this post blurs responsibility, ups costs, fosters subordinate politicking, adds yet another layer, and usually frustrates the deputies themselves. Squeezing the size of staff organizations to the core is wise since they are not profit centers. Indeed their purpose is to help those in the line organizations achieve their assigned goals. This fact is lost among the corporate staff in all too many organizations.

Each organizational level creates a need for approval and coordination. The more levels, the more time and energy sapped by these efforts, and the more openings for bureaucratic veto-ers or "Abominable No-Men." For a governmental or large corporate organization to have ten or more layers, as they often do, encourages stagnation, delay, and difficulty in getting the word out effectively. Expanding managers' span of control to at least a dozen or so employees helps limit the number of layers in the organization and increases agility. It also keeps managers busy and discourages dabbling by those who won't delegate.

While drawing an organization chart merits much effort and thought, drawing up a reorganization chart demands even more and should be avoided in most cases. Too often, redrawing an organization chart is simply a means of giving the impression of action while disregarding the fundamental problems that plague the organization in the first place. The essentials of a good organization are described (and naturally ascribed to divine wisdom) by the Bishop of Canterbury in *Henry V:* "Therefore doth heaven divide the state of man in divers functions, setting endeavour in continual motion." Each organization, he says, must be "fixed" with "an aim."

LESSON FOUR

"God give thee the spirit of persuasion and him
the ears of profiting, that what thou speakest may
move, and what he hears may be believed."
—Falstaff, in *Henry IV, Part I*

The modern executive must penetrate today's entertainment and information barrage to get the corporate message out to all its various constituencies, including stockholders, employees, customers, the media, government officials, special interest groups, community leaders, and more. Each of them needs fast, accurate information and they all want it first. Effective communication thus becomes far more complex than it was for Antony at Caesar's funeral, where his brilliant speech to an audience within eyeball range turned the flow of the day's events and ultimately changed history.

To reach these constituencies there is now a vast array of communication devices, from conventional word-of-mouth rumor mills to unsolicited blast-faxes, e-mails, voice mail, Web pages, and videos.

Modern executives must ensure that the message works effectively. The stakes are high. Shakespeare shows the tremendous power of communications throughout *Julius Caesar,* where words determine the fate of the key characters, and of Rome itself. While respecting public opinion, the Bard is well aware of its subjectivity. The wise Cicero, when commenting on the "strange-disposed time," mentions that perceptions may be more important than hard facts: "Men may construe things after their fashion, clean [distinct] from the purpose of the things themselves."

Antony furnishes several lessons that apply to effective communications today:

1. Know the topic cold. This is expected of any top executive, but in the normal course of business some particulars of an issue may be unfamiliar. To best prepare for an internal or public presentation, the executive and staff should anticipate the questions most likely to be asked after a speech or during an interview—especially those the executive most wants to avoid—and prepare the best answer for each one. If more than 10 percent of the actual questions weren't on the list, there is a problem far more serious than communications.

2. Arrange the setting and prepare carefully. Many executives are more comfortable sitting behind a desk than standing on a podium. When delivering a speech, they can "quake and change . . . colour," or, as Richard III says, "murder thy breath in middle of a word, and then again begin, and stop again, as if thou were distraught and mad with terror."

A "murder board" of key insiders and a trusted outsider or two can help prepare the speaker for the all-important question period. A practice drill, during which the presenter is asked tough questions, can help clarify the issues and increase the speaker's confidence.

3. *Be crisp, frank, interesting, and understated.* So inundated is the listener today that an executive's message cannot break through if not well presented. Brutus does a respectable job at Caesar's funeral, but Antony steals the show.

A speech need not be extensive to be engaging. As the boy says in *Henry V,* "Men of few words are the best men" and speeches of the fewest possible words are often the best speeches. Being crisp requires being clear beforehand on precisely what the message will be, and keeping that message simple.

Being frank is essential for credibility, which in turn is imperative if the audience is to accept the message. While few executives can be as provocative as Antony, they nonetheless can do better than just stand there dourly in a gray suit and mumble through footnotes in the annual report.

The company's business reports should flow from the facts. Even in tough times, executives should aim to underpromise and overdeliver. Too many managers resemble the description by Cressida in *Troilus and Cressida*—who warns against those who "swear more performance than they are able." They have a habit of "vowing more than the perfection of ten and discharging less than the tenth part of one."

Finally, bad news should never be delivered on the installment plan. Tell how bad it could turn out to be one time, and then pledge to do better next time. Credibility is a priceless asset, one extraordinarily difficult to restore, if restorable at all. It should not be eroded by hype. No matter how enjoyable the rush of news after a hyped announcement, "in the end, truth will out" as Launcelot says in *The Merchant of Venice*.

4. Avoid giving "no comment" or going "off the record." These two common responses are usually ill advised.

"No comment" or "I haven't read the indictment" should be relegated to last resort in a truly perilous situation—and preferably shunned even then. Once employed, the phrase becomes a drug, which may turn habitual. Not only is it easy to dispense, but it also often becomes harmful to the dispenser as well as the consumer. Even when a substantive answer would be helpful, the spokesperson must offer a "no comment" on other aspects of an issue previously handled in this way. The company cannot give a "no comment" to true "rumors" while emphatically denying false ones.

Likewise, going "off the record" with the media, customers, employees, and others, however popular and tempting, is almost always unwise. Executives unwilling to say something for the record probably shouldn't say anything at all. Unwanted television appearances can easily be refused, or accepted only on the condition that they be "live." With lots of videotape chasing little airtime, an edited broadcast of a lengthier interview can create all kinds of problems. Of course, a "live" performance can also create undesirable surprises. The executive in demand must assess his relevant strengths and weaknesses, then chose a venue accordingly.

5. *Go hi-tech.* As Antony demonstrated, the oldest means of communications, face to face, is still the best. But with audiences now scattered around the world, face to face has become nearly impossible for many corporations.

The second oldest means, a written memorandum, ranks with the worst. Not only is it impersonal, but it also discourages the give-and-take necessary for sound decision-making. Besides, executives in large corporations and government agencies can become so inundated by memos that they ignore them out of frustration. Moreover, written memos lack the impact of more personal and direct communications. "To see sad sights," Shakespeare writes in his poem "The Rape of Lucrece," "moves more than to hear them told."

Modern means of communication, amazing as they are, work amazingly well. E-mail excels because of its speed, ease of use, and targeted distribution; Web sites because of their wide distribution and links to other information sources; videoconferencing because it can connect distant participants personally and visually in actual time; and cell phones by making callers accessible to one another from nearly any location.

6. *Prepare for leaks.* There are times companies need to communicate and times when they need to not communicate. Executives should avoid, even in allegedly

private meetings, saying what they wouldn't want to read the next day in the press. Many high-level and otherwise perceptive officials and executives have been fired for side comments to "loyal" associates or in the presence of what they believed was a dead microphone or, worse yet, in the case of Prince Hal, in the presence of what he presumed was a dead king.

Employees need to be reminded of the importance of confidentiality in certain business circumstances, such as dealing with possible mergers and acquisitions, new product plans, and personnel matters. Photocopiers and cell phones have been a disaster for corporate security, the latter less from a standpoint of technical interception than simply from careless use.

While taking all possible steps to prevent unwanted disclosures, it is wise to develop a contingency plan ready to go into effect should a leak occur. Anyone assuming everything will leak is usually not disappointed.

Business communications, while essential, are both tricky and treacherous. The unfortunately named Fool, in his temporary role as King Lear's spokesperson, said what many of his future colleagues today feel: "They'll have me whipped for speaking true. Thou will have me whipped for lying. And sometimes I am whipped for holding my peace."

LESSON FIVE
"Beware the Ides of March!"

—Soothsayer, in *Julius Caesar*

As was true in the time of Julius Caesar, and is still true today, executives must attend to detail and act with the utmost discipline and diligence if they are to get the job done. But at the same time, as we have repeatedly seen, they must be good at dealing with people. The best executives avoid being accused of "the truth you speak . . . lacks some gentleness and time to speak it in. You rub the sore when you should bring the plaster," as Gonzalo says in *The Tempest*.

Global competition is so stiff, the regulatory environment so onerous, stockholder and employee expectations so high, stockholders' class-action lawyers so opportunistic, and customers so demanding that few executives reach the heights. The Julius Caesars of the business world rarely come across the world's stage.

Antony gains steadily throughout the play—not because he is most perceptive, intelligent, or skilled—but because he is the best communicator and most attentive to details. After Brutus permits him to speak at Caesar's funeral, Antony realizes the enormous consequences that can flow from a seemingly small mistake.

This happens in virtually all realms. The Space Shuttle *Challenger* blew up in 1986 because some small pieces of a rubbery seal didn't work on a chilly day. A spacecraft launched to explore the planets was last spotted heading toward the sun because a programmer neglected to insert a hyphen in one of the tens of thousands of lines of software code aboard that spacecraft. These grandiose projects do "in the general censure, take corruption from that [one] particular fault," as Hamlet says.

A number of small insurance companies were allegedly victimized in 1999 by Martin Frankel, a financier accused of using money he was supposed to invest on their behalf in wire fraud and money laundering. Frankel, who went by several aliases, had been involved with a charity associated with the Vatican. This blinded the insurance executives to signs, which, had they been more attentive to details, would have warned them that something was wrong. It is reported that he went on the lam with an estimated $215 million belonging to the insurance companies. Frankel, who lived lavishly in a mansion in Greenwich, Connecticut, was the type who could "wet my cheeks with artificial tears and frame my face to all occasions," as Gloucester says in *Henry IV, Part III.*

J. C. Penney chief executive James E. Oesterreicher has been criticized for failing to pay adequate attention to important factors that have redefined the retail world. After years of flat earnings, Oesterreicher recently made some bold moves, investing $300 million in remodeling stores and $75 million into retailing on the Internet. But J. C. Penney is being squeezed from above and below. Higher-end merchandisers have lowered their prices in order to poach customers. At the same time, stores like Target and Old Navy can offer hipper merchandise at lower prices. Penney's management paid too little attention for too long to creeping changes that harmed its competitive position.

In carrying out a task one must constantly be on the lookout for signals that corrective actions are needed. The most highly prized recruit, Brutus, proves a calamity once on the conspiratorial team. His mind is closed to all thoughts and ideas except his own, which aren't sound. Even though Cassius has a deft feel for a situation, he becomes powerless as Brutus constantly ignores his advice.

The Perkin-Elmer Corporation refused to believe that the huge mirror it built for the Hubble space telescope was improperly shaped. The management discounted one test that showed a gross error, ordered another kind of test, and then dismissed that one, too. Only after the telescope relayed blurry pictures from space in 1990 did Perkin-Elmer recognize its enormous error. The correction, a pair of space "spectacles," was costly but possible. When the device was installed by some fly-by astronauts, the outer-space Mr. Magoo turned into a technological wizard.

Besides using their ears to listen better, management should use a "red team" to better see potential problems in execution. A good red team challenges every critical action at every critical step.

Many a promising career has suddenly turned unpromising when a seemingly small error, often caused by neglect of some detail, brought about large damage. The careers of both Brutus and Cassius plummeted when they fell prey to one seemingly small error: letting Antony speak. Shakespeare told this unforgiving truth in Sonnet 25: "The painful warrior, famous for fight after a thousand victories, once foiled, is from the book of honor razed." His career crashes after that one foil, "and all the rest forgot for which he toiled."

By the same token, it is important to beware of those who would undermine your business goals using their own rules of the game. Commercial espionage, for instance, is booming in many parts of the business world. Care must be taken to protect technological breakthroughs, marketing plans, new product ideas, and research programs.

The danger is particularly acute in countries with less-developed codes of business ethics. In fact, in some of these countries commercial bribes are legal—and even tax-deductible. In one case, when more ethical executives protested such practices, the foreign officials said that future bribes by its nationals would be tax-deductible *only* with prior government approval.

Having set a firm foundation, leaders have the opportunity to exemplify the type of determination that set Caesar apart as one of history's truly great men. The power of determination, both to accomplish deeds and to set an example, is perhaps best propounded in *King John*, when His Majesty says:

> Be stirring as the time. Be fire with fire.
> Threaten the threatener, and outface the brow
> Of bragging horror; so shall inferior eyes,
> That borrow their behaviours from the great,
> Grow great by your example, and put on
> the dauntless spirit of resolution.

ACT IV

RISK MANAGEMENT

"Who Chooseth Me Must

Give and Hazard All He Hath"

[DRAMATIS EXECUTIVUS SUMMARIUS]

Shakespeare's only play named for a businessman, *The Merchant of Venice,* stresses the need to take on risk.

While accepting risk is an element of life, choosing it is an essential element of corporate success. Business is, after all, risky. The potential for loss permeates its every aspect. The stock market is the very embodiment of uncertainty. Doing business also entails making decisions under uncertain conditions. A company reluctant "to give and hazard" in the marketplace can often be bettered by a competitor who is willing to do so.

Still, the fact that executives continually confront risk doesn't mean they must blindly accept whatever it brings. Risk can be prudently managed, much as Portia, the heroine of this Act, shows so masterfully.

Unlike most contemporary plays or other artistic creations, *The Merchant of Venice* extols business and shows respect for corporate executives and admiration for commerce in general. Within its story are sharp examples needed by every businessperson who has asked, "When should I take a risk—and how can I best manage it?"

PROLOGUE

A play full of merchants and people treated like merchandise, *The Merchant of Venice* highlights the character of Portia. Like Rosalind in *As You Like It*, Viola in *Twelfth Night*, Helena in *All's Well That Ends Well*, and Juliet in *Romeo and Juliet*, Portia vastly overshadows her male counterparts.

As the play opens, Portia, who lives a very cushy life on a country estate, tries to cope with boredom. However, when the opportunity to take chances and overcome obstacles presents itself, she comes alive and achieves great success.

Her decisions swirl around choosing a husband and then saving the life of his best friend Antonio, the merchant of Venice himself. A successful businessman, Antonio nonetheless makes a particularly risky move when he borrows money from Shylock, the local moneylender.

The treatment of the complex Shylock offers a startling and disturbing look into one of life's darkest corners. *The Merchant of Venice,* more than any other of Shakespeare's plays, explores such volatile issues as anti-Semitism and racial prejudice, ethnic stereotyping, and gender restrictions. It examines the role of the outsider, who is feared and yet needed, living in a homogenous, commercial society. Bristling at the outrages he must endure, Shylock longs for revenge against the bigoted establishment that tortures him. When Antonio comes to him to borrow funds, Shylock gets his chance.

Quite apart from its religious and social dimensions, this controversial play displays brilliant understanding of the riskiness of business. Ultimately it probes into the depths of managing risks not only in commerce but in life. For Portia, that means taking on nothing less than traditions and laws, friendship and marriage, and, most crucially, life and death.

Scene I

[Curtain rises. Enter elegant lady of the manor, fanning herself and chatting with attendant.]

One of the beautiful people of the greater Venetian area, wealthy Portia faces another boring day in paradise. "By my troth, Nerissa, my little body is aweary of this great world," she sighs to her attendant.

Nerissa, to her credit, cuts her lady no slack. "You would be [aweary], sweet madam," she replies with more sarcasm than sympathy, "if your miseries were in the same abundance as your good fortunes are."

Meanwhile, back in the city, well-to-do Antonio also

has a bad case of the blues despite the fact that his venture capitalism has gone global. Unfortunately Antonio's far-flung assets drain his liquidity, which is now needed to help his best friend, Bassanio. A man ahead of his time, Bassanio activates the concept of risking OPM—other people's money. Already having borrowed heaps from Antonio, he requires still more heaps.

The personification of the irresponsible risk-taker, Bassanio needs cash to settle old debts and launch a new venture. He tells Antonio, "In Belmont is a lady richly left. Her name is Portia—nothing undervalued." Should Bassanio's arrow land there he would "questionless be fortunate."

However, as is the case with many venture capitalists, Antonio's liquidity clumps more than it flows. "Thou knowest that all my fortunes are at sea. Neither have I money nor commodity to raise a present sum," he laments to Bassanio as he seeks to float the equivalent of commercial paper.

Nonetheless, for such a special friend, the risk-taker will "try what my credit can in Venice" to underwrite the wooing. In his straitened circumstances, Antonio can borrow money only from a Jew like Shylock, who has loads of ducats to lend.

Shylock, however, despises Antonio, not only for his anti-Semitism but also because, by law, Antonio must lend money interest-free, thereby curtailing Shylock's market. So Shylock concocts a novel notion: Antonio must repay the loan on the exact date due or else have "an equal pound of your fair flesh to be cut off and taken in what part of your body pleaseth me."

While business requires taking risks, it doesn't mean taking stupid ones. Antonio should heed the terms-and-conditions clauses in a contract; ignoring the terms has sunk many a gifted executive after him. Previously Antonio controls risk well by diversifying: "My ventures are not in one bottom trusted, nor to one place. Nor is my whole estate upon the fortune of this present year." This is a sound business practice as long as the diversification isn't in an area where the diversifier lacks experience.

Here, on a personal matter, Antonio agrees to Shylock's narrow but deep hole, wherein the risk is judged minimal but the consequences of failure are clearly maximal. Nor does he lay off part of the risk by seeking some form of business-interruption insurance.

Back in Belmont, Portia longs for her own bond—of marriage. Unfortunately this quintessential Renaissance lady is plagued by a dead though still domineering father. She can "neither choose who I would, nor refuse who I dislike" because of restrictions her father has placed on her.

His will stipulates that a suitor must solve a riddle and choose among three closed caskets—one of lead, one of silver, and the third of gold (the metals of commerce) to win Portia. If a suitor picks the right casket, he gets Portia "with her sunny locks [that] hang on her temples like a golden fleece" as well as her golden trust fund. But if he fails, he must never "woo a maid in way of marriage" again. It is truly a risky business.

Portia must untangle the mess her father has devised if she is to get married, a situation that resembles mergers and acquisitions today. Both combine high risks and high stakes: more than a third of all marriages in this country fail, as do more than two-thirds of all mergers and acquisitions. Those that beat the odds do so through synergy, which is easier to anticipate than to realize.

Little does Portia realize what big risks lie ahead, both at home and in Venice. The intriguing way she manages them proves instructive.

SCENE II

[Enter lonely lady meditating on three closed caskets, with notes atop each.]

To achieve her goal of marriage, Portia begins to manage risk prudently and competently. This is not surprising given her brains and spunk, but is rather startling given that she is a woman in a male-dominated society. Still, she acts like a top executive and proceeds as if her will and skill matter more than her position, and she assumes her executive posture by outlining her plan for the forthcoming joint venture.

First, she aims to marry someone who can fit in, but not take over, Belmont. Second, she identifies all available options. She learns of several wannabe suitors, and then proceeds to the third and fourth stages of sound decision-making—collecting facts and analyzing options.

Some gentleman callers turn out to lack the technical skills needed to function as her lord. Portia dismisses one chap since he "hath neither Latin, French, nor Italian"; evidently there's a language requirement for admission to Belmont. Another fellow drinks too much. "I will do anything, Nerissa, [before] I will be married to a sponge," Portia says, clearly implying that she will somehow choose, despite the parental will.

And so she does. She rejects other potential husbands because they would clash with the corporate culture. Belmont has its own style and manner, just as contemporary companies have their own personalities, behavior patterns, and reputations, all of which are set largely at the top.

The Prince of Morocco arrives, resplendent in his all-white robe, and immediately addresses the issue of his race in all-white Belmont. His first words to Portia are: "Mislike me not for my complexion," and he tells her with panache that the sun shines so brightly in northern Africa that it darkens the skin.

The problem quickly becomes moot once he, fittingly, chooses the glitzy gold casket whose riddle reads, "Who chooseth me shall gain what many men desire." This is the wrong choice, because to Portia's father, love entails more than just desire or a pile of gold.

Another prince arrives, this one from Arragon. Talkative and foppish, he chooses the silver casket, which says, "Who chooseth me shall get as much as he deserves." This prince sees his potential portfolio crash, too.

The tension rises as a butler breathlessly announces that "a young Venetian," Bassanio, has "alighted" at the gate. Even before appearing, Bassanio has carefully structured his venture. Aware that preparation counts in any commercial transaction, he's already shipped "gifts of rich value" to pique Portia's passion. The elegantly attired fellow figures this will lead straight to the woman's heart, but he may have miscalculated. For, among all the characters in this play, Portia is the only one in possession of a full treasury. On the other hand, the gifts indicate that he knows how to behave properly in upscale Belmont. Most of all, Bassanio realizes that wedding Portia would end his big cash-flow woes, and lounging around her grand estate would be a dream come true. But he must choose the right casket.

However, Portia must first make *her* decision, which delivers yet another lesson in handling a risky project. She recognizes that it is wise, in any competitive situation like this, to determine an acceptable outcome before the bidding war stimulates too many personal passions. One of the most common errors in bidding wars is to get caught up in the spirit of the chase.

As Portia realizes, emotions must be contained, especially when the action starts. Like any wise executive in a complicated situation, she works on her self-control. When, a bit later, she feels her "passions" rise and a "shuddering fear," she strains to get a grip: "O love, be moderate," she counsels herself.

Portia has met Bassanio once before and was taken with him then. He may not be the ideal husband, but, as happens so often in business, he is the best available option. Also, there exists the possibility of a certain amount of restructuring. Portia knows he is "a scholar and a soldier," but she lacks essential information about his character, although that, too, is common in commerce. At decision time, an executive usually finds fewer facts than factors, each with its own probability of accuracy. Uncertainty reigns.

Uncertainty notwithstanding, she practices insightful executive recruitment, wherein a person's strongest trait—or even an average of all his or her attributes—does not determine his or her ultimate potential. Rather, the weakest of the person's relevant qualities defines his or her limitations.

Applying this principle, which carries over into modern-day headhunting, Portia finds that Bassanio's feeblest traits are fairly negligible or at least manageable. Moreover, as the top bachelor in the greater Belmont area, he's the best option around. Well spoken and well titled, Bassanio is already a lord and would make an elegant host of Belmont. And he wants the job.

Though fiscally irresponsible, Bassanio is basically honest. Above all, he has a sunny disposition and a conciliatory nature. He constantly states his preference on matters that arise in the play, only to have it consistently overturned, or, more often, simply ignored, by others. He's comfortable in a subordinate role, which suits Portia's executive temperament just fine. He would make an excellent special assistant to the head of the company.

Moreover, while Bassanio may not be the ideal Mr. Right, he is Mr. Here. Portia chooses him, and now she must overcome daunting obstacles to get him through the confounding human-resource-approval system her father established. For starters, she must ascertain that he really does want her, not just her assets. "I pray you tarry," she greets him, as if Bassanio had anywhere else to go, and then she tells him boldly, "I would not lose you."

For his part, Bassanio realizes his own limitations and wants her to "teach me answers for deliverance." Portia's velvet-gloved leadership now begins. Given her father's will, she must manage the risk indirectly. "Let music sound while he doth make his choice," Portia orders. This strongly hints of her help, since songs were commonly used to convey messages. The selection, with its clear theme of the dangers of "fancy," could help Bassanio eliminate the fanciest gold casket, and perhaps the shiny silver one as well. As in most business correspondence, it is necessary to read between the lines.

Second, the song urges everyone to disregard outward appearances and closes with another hint contained in the lyric, "Ding, dong, bell." Bells are seldom made of gold or silver, yet commonly contain lead.

But Portia, who must have planned all this out beforehand, figures that even those hints may escape Bassanio's notice. But he can't miss how the lines of the song end with "bed," "head," "fed," and two other rhyming words. Now, even Bassanio may think, "Duh, it's lead!"

Compliant as always, Bassanio chooses the lead casket, the one that says, "Who chooseth me must give and hazard all he hath." For Bassanio that's not much of a sacrifice, but for his two lovers, Antonio and Portia, it holds great portent.

In the brief interlude of joy, Portia celebrates getting her man and Bassanio celebrates getting her money. Free at last of her father's control, the quick-witted lady can continue to reign as she pleases. Right after becoming engaged, Portia shapes their relationship by handing Bassanio an engagement ring. Gently she reiterates the deal: "Since you are dear bought, I will love you dear."

Soon thereafter some of Bassanio's Venetian friends show up bearing bad news from the business front. They report that Antonio has "all his ventures failed." The distressing news "steals the color from Bassanio's cheek."

Portia becomes concerned. After hearing that Antonio's debt is three thousand ducats, she makes a mistake common among neophyte executives and throws money at the problem. "Pay him six thousand," she commands. If that won't do, then "double six thousand and then treble that," she suggests. As in most corporate instances, that approach won't solve the problem; it will merely increase the magnitude of the disaster.

Still, Portia's talk of money reminds Bassanio of that touchy topic. He has been holding back a little item of bad news, a luxury few contemporary companies enjoy, though many attempt it. In business, problems and failures are best told fast and fully. Bad news dribbled out on the installment plan only makes a difficult situation worse. Yet many executives have trouble appreciating the ways in which the so-called coverup is usually worse than the problem itself. Furthermore, a coverup denies people in the company the opportunity to try to solve the problem.

Finally Bassanio comes clean. "When I did first impart my love to you," he tells his new fiancée, "I freely told you all the wealth I had ran in my veins: I was a gentleman. And yet, dear lady, rating myself at nothing, you shall see how much I was a braggart." He actually "should then have told you that I was worse than nothing." He had borrowed "to feed my means" from Antonio, who in turn borrowed from Shylock— and a pound of Antonio's supple flesh is now at risk.

Bassanio wishes to race to Antonio's side. Even in this panicky moment in Belmont, which is not normally a crisis center, Portia keeps her priorities straight. She tells her charging-off fiancé to hold tight a minute. "First go with me to church and call me wife, and then away to Venice to your friend," she instructs him, trying to turn the dicey situation into some form of a win-win.

After a quick wedding, Bassanio gets ready to return to "the dearest friend to me, the kindest man, the best-conditioned and unwearied spirit," the new groom tells his bride. Portia understands that her husband, having risked the life of his dearest friend, must "give and hazard all he hath" to save him—or at least part of him.

Like any successful executive, one of Portia's greatest assets is her keen insight into other people's strengths and weaknesses. Instantly she grasps that Bassanio will never be able to save Antonio—only she can.

But how? She's been married some ten minutes and aware of the bond for little more. As a woman, she is confined to her estate and not expected to know affairs of state. She has met neither Antonio nor Shylock, knows little of their contract, and surely never studied law. Nonetheless, rather than hire outside legal counsel, she decides to take on the case herself.

The odds of success are low, the dangers high, and the solution hard to fathom. In short, it is everything Portia longed for as she whiled away her time in the idyllic countryside. Like all able executives, she doesn't shirk from challenges. Indeed, she welcomes them. There is nothing like a positive attitude, whether in business or in life, to help assure a positive outcome.

So, to face a new series of risks, she hastens to the city. But to do what once she gets there?

Scene III

[Enter young lady in traveling clothes with assistant, looking for her butler.]

Portia immediately organizes her minimal staff. She runs a lean machine with very little overhead, at least on the road. She orders the butler to deliver a letter to a cousin in Padua. Once there, he'll hand him "notes and garments." Then the butler is to meet her at the ferry crossing into Venice.

Portia, like any first-rate executive, understands that even in the best-managed endeavors, things sometimes go wrong. But by now she's learned that little that Bassanio does is well managed, so things will almost always go wrong.

She has also realized that Antonio has allowed his life to become endangered by falling prey to both types of mishaps common to any risky venture.

First, Antonio suffers from "known unknowns" or accidents which, however improbable, are not inconceivable and should be avoidable. For example, all of his ships could conceivably be lost at sea. Multiple mishaps, like not having fully seaworthy ships and sending them all to the same place at the same time, could cause a major loss; a single problem is rarely the cause of most disasters. Major catastrophes usually occur when several seemingly unrelated problems arise simultaneously.

Second, Antonio falls victim to "unknown unknowns" or factors that could not have been imagined but happen nonetheless. This category is by far the most dangerous to well-managed companies.

A series of unimaginable events change what Shylock initially called a "merry jest" into a deadly deal. Shylock's only child, Jessica, elopes with an anti-Semitic Christian and announces that she plans to convert to Christianity. This leaves the moneylender devastated and alone in a hostile world. Crueler yet, she absconds with some of his money and jewels, including the ring he had bestowed upon Leah, his beloved late wife. Then, while coping with crushing grief, Shylock is taunted in the street by two brownshirts named Salario and Solanio, who happen to be friends of Antonio.

With mounting ferocity, Shylock feels what he had previously called "the ancient grudge I bear him" for centuries of persecution of Jews and years of personal abuse. At the time of the loan negotiation, Shylock had reminded Antonio, "You call me misbeliever, cut-throat dog, and spit upon my Jewish gabardine." Antonio admitted such behavior and, just to ensure no misunderstanding, insulted Shylock once more: "I am as like to call thee so again, to spit on thee again, to spurn thee too."

Something snaps in Shylock's psyche, and he decides

to make Antonio pay for his own Job-like suffering. He decides that he *will* demand that pound of flesh. The conceivable but highly unlikely danger has become real. As in business, people who speak without thinking have a way of making a bad situation worse.

Antonio must recognize the danger he is in, but still he does not act. Instead of functioning like an executive, Antonio languishes as a doomed victim. Bassanio, likewise, does nothing, primarily because he *can* do nothing; it is beyond his capability. Only Portia can overcome these great hurdles, but she is nowhere in sight as the dramatic courtroom scene begins.

The presiding Duke has already appealed to Shylock for mercy, but he won't settle out of court. The Duke then pleads for justice, which evokes a scathing response from Shylock. How, he demands, can a person call for justice when, "you have among you many a purchased slave." Instead, Shylock insists upon the letter of the law. The bond with Antonio is legal; it was agreed, written, and now must be enforced.

Suddenly Portia enters the courtroom. She is dressed as a young male lawyer and is accompanied by a clerk (actually Nerissa). Portia first says that she has become "informed thoroughly" on the issues. She asks Antonio to "confess" the bond. He does so, and she concludes simply, "Then must the Jew be merciful" to avoid killing Antonio for not making the precise loan repayment at the exact time due.

Shylock lashes back at her, demanding, "On what compulsion must I? Tell me that."

And, out flows one of the most marvelous speeches

ever written. Portia is at her best when she points out that, "The quality of mercy is not strained. It droppeth as the gentle rain from heaven upon the place beneath." In fact, mercy is "mightiest in the mightiest" as it "becomes the thronèd monarch better than his crown." While a scepter indicates a king's earthly power, mercy stands above that. "It is enthronèd in the hearts of kings. It is an attribute to God himself." The powerful on earth show themselves most like God "when mercy seasons justice."

Thus Portia closes the greatest opening argument in courtroom history, especially by a lawyer who never passed the bar. She also begins to lay a trap by telling Shylock that he can win his case, that the court must enforce law and therefore "must needs give sentence 'gainst the merchant there."

This is an odd argument from a defense attorney, but it delights Shylock, who cries, "My deeds upon my head. I crave the law." Bassanio then offers Shylock double the amount owed, which Shylock refuses. Bassanio then implores the Duke to fudge the law: "I beseech you, wrest once the law to your authority. To do a great right, do a little wrong," by refusing to enforce the bond.

Like any able risk manager, Portia grasps the big picture. Bassanio's "little wrong" would set a devastating precedent by bending the law upon which Venetian business is based. The city started and flourished as a trading center and could not continue to thrive without a solid legal system to protect its commerce. Far-thinking Portia responds sharply, telling Bassanio, "It cannot be."

But what "can be" is narrowing. Portia gives Shylock another chance by upping the amount of money thrown at the problem: "Take thrice thy money; bid me tear the bond." He answers, "By my soul, I swear there is no power in the tongue of man to alter me."

Portia then asks Antonio to "lay bare your bosom." Shylock has brought a scale to weigh the pound he'll slice from the defendant. But Shylock has brought nothing to stop Antonio from bleeding to death. When asked why not, Shylock says that it isn't in the bond. Portia, deftly turning a liability into an asset, points out that decency demands it.

Portia's trap is about to snap shut. As Shylock sharpens his knife, Portia makes a small request. "Tarry a little," she says softly. "There is something else."

Until now, Shylock has managed all the "known unknowns" in his predicament. He surely anticipated the sundry pleas for mercy, for justice, and the offer of bribes. But he could not have predicted the legal intricacies of the "unknown unknowns."

Portia now points out that Venetian law penalizes any "alien," including Jews, who shed "Christian blood," which is obviously the only type Antonio has. The bond allows Shylock to take one pound of flesh, but "in the cutting it, if thou dost shed one drop of Christian blood, thy lands and goods are, by the laws of Venice, confiscated unto the state."

Suddenly the courtroom mood lifts. "Is that the law?" Shylock falters. Portia shows him the statute. Okay, he concedes, he "*will* take this offer then" of three times the bond and let Antonio live.

Bassanio joyfully shrieks, "Here is the money!" but again Portia nixes him and clamps the snare tighter still. Should Shylock take any more or less than one pound of flesh he will violate the agreement and thus must "diest and all thy goods are confiscated."

Hearing this, the courtroom crowd cheers as Shylock sinks lower. "Give me my principal, and let me go," he pleads. Bassanio, happy to comply, flings it over. Portia, as expected, blocks it. Beaten, Shylock says he'll simply walk away and forget the whole sick business.

In response, another soft but piercing, "Tarry, Jew" comes from Portia. She explains that Shylock has already violated the law "against an alien that . . . seeks the life of any citizen." The penalty is forfeiture of half the alien's goods to the Christian threatened and half to the state. The violator even faces capital punishment, should the Duke so order.

With this pronouncement, the courtroom turns positively nasty. "Down therefore," Portia orders Shylock, "and beg mercy of the Duke." Before he does so, the Duke offers to spare Shylock's life.

Then Portia reiterates the appropriateness of confiscating all of Shylock's goods, and, not surprisingly, he objects. To him, taking his lands and goods is like taking his livelihood and his life.

Now the relieved Antonio makes a seemingly generous, but in fact vicious, offer. He'll forgo receiving half of Shylock's goods if the Jew leaves them to "the gentleman that lately stole his daughter." Then he recommends that Shylock "presently become a Christian" and explicitly gift all his possessions to his converted daughter. The Duke concurs with this and orders Shylock to act accordingly. Otherwise he'll rescind the pardon on Shylock's life.

This cascade of cataclysmic rulings so floors Shylock he can only gasp, "Send the deed after me, and I will sign it." He slinks away, utterly defeated, a victim of both known and unknown circumstances that lead to personal ruin. In the business world, stubborn insistence and uncompromising positions work contrary to resolving problems. Compromise, the heart of accord, is essential when addressing business parameters.

The fate of Shylock is so dramatically bitter that it is easy to overlook how well Portia manages a high-risk situation and saves a life. She knows what she wants, has done her homework, tries to work out a cooperative solution, and understands the other side's emotional issues. Thoughtful, she doesn't seek an instant solution. Respectful, she calls on the Duke to mediate when appropriate. Above all else, she is persistent.

Antonio, has more management experience and much more at stake, but doesn't manage the situation at all. The Duke has more legal experience, but cannot devise a compromise acceptable to all parties. Others have more civic involvement (Portia doesn't even live in Venice) but don't see the high stakes inherent in the sanctity of Venetian law. Only Portia bears all these attributes, and, by the trial's close, it is her awareness of the fine points of the law that matter.

Portia works within the conventions of her society. However objectionable the social mores imposed upon her, she outwardly conforms to the extent she must. She is no rebel but she'll have her way, even if it takes some subterfuge as well as meticulous and inspired thinking. For successful executives, achieving results always requires hard work.

After her stellar courtroom success, Portia scurries back to Belmont, where she bestows good news like some fairy godmother at Christmastime. To Antonio, she gives the surprising but welcome tidings that his ships have mysteriously come safely into port after all. She informs Jessica and Lorenzo that they'll reap Shylock's inheritance. And she proclaims to Bassanio that she won't deny him "anything I have—no, not my body nor my husband's bed."

A chance-taker who never falters, Portia exemplifies extraordinary risk management.

ACTING LESSONS

Portia offers executives six very basic lessons on dealing with risk, including the legitimacy of its role, weighing alternative options, dealing with intangibles, acting dispassionately, not wagering everything, and managing a risk once it is accepted.

LESSON ONE

"They lose that do buy it with [too]
much care."

—Gratiano, in *The Merchant of Venice*

Any corporate executive interested in thriving, or even surviving, must encourage risk-taking. The riskiest course of all is refusing to do so.

Portia takes huge risks and achieves success as a result. Today's corporate executives must, to survive in our fast-moving business climate, take risks as well. Otherwise their organizations will turn bureaucratic and cautious and consequently atrophy. Employees will sense that if they do everything in the ordinary way, everything will be fine. Once management piles enough risk-averse bureaucrats on top of one another, disaster is no longer left to chance.

Even Bill Gates has been known to say that Microsoft is two years away from failure. If his business model falls behind the marketplace, he's finished. If business opportunities are not seized, they may be gone. "Who seeks, and will not take when once 'tis offered shall never find it more," Menas points out in *Antony and Cleopatra*.

Today's corporate leaders can encourage risk-taking by welcoming new, even unsettling, ideas. The Duke of Venice, bland as he is, takes a chance when he allows a young, unknown attorney to take over a major case in his courtroom.

Second, managers must tolerate failures. Those who don't fall short every once in a while are not stretching, either themselves or their teams, to go beyond ordinary activities into extraordinary challenges and successes. A manager unwilling to accept occasional defeat should find a new line of work.

While failures in results must occasionally be accepted by corporate management, failures caused by indifference, neglect, or poor judgment should not be. Nor should managers tolerate surprises; they should remain aware of all factors affecting their projects and carefully monitor progress and gauge the odds of any setbacks.

Finally, to foster risk-taking, top executives should guide the corporate auditors to help rather than merely hunt. Auditors should become active, constructive overseers who foster the success of the operating units, rather than suspicious inspectors frantic to find fraud, abuse, and failure.

One company that has thrived as a result of its risk-taking is AT&T. When chairman and CEO C. Michael Armstrong left Hughes Electronics in November 1997 to take the helm of the huge telecommunications conglomerate, the company had become slow-moving, bureaucratic, and mired in its past life as a utility. Armstrong knew some risk-taking was essential. "We have seen better days," says the Duke Senior in *As You Like It*, which was precisely the sentiment of Wall Street analysts about AT&T.

Armstrong took a series of gutsy steps to position AT&T as a complete global communications provider. One major step was to buy Tele-Communications Inc., the cable TV powerhouse, in March 1999. The idea was to sell local telephone and high-speed data services over that firm's widespread cable network. Coupled with an alliance with Time Warner, that bold move gave AT&T a direct route into two-thirds of American homes.

Previously it lacked such extensive access because the local phone lines linking homes to long-distance carriers like AT&T were controlled by local Baby Bell companies. AT&T's earnings per share grew 25 percent in 1998, and net income was up 37.9 percent. Since Armstrong took the reins, the share price has increased more than 70 percent.

Encouraging risk-taking means tolerating and then overcoming failure. When John Bello, founder of South Beach Beverage Co., started selling iced-tea drinks in 1995, his product line went sour and the company struggled to pay off its $2 million debt. Bello, a former PepsiCo executive and ex-president of NFL Properties, resisted going out of business.

Instead, he used his house as collateral on another $1 million loan and in 1997 introduced a trendy product line, SoBe, which includes healthy drinks spiked with ginkgo and ginseng. It wasn't the type of product one would expect from a fifty-three-year-old corporate executive, but it enticed his target audience of hip, youthful consumers. Bello's willingness to take risk and start over paid off, as South Beach sales skyrocketed from $2.1 million in 1996 to $67 million in 1998.

The Internet auction site eBay was launched despite a slew of jumbo risks and great uncertainties. Would bidders honor their bids? Would sellers accurately describe their wares? Would anyone care? The risk-averse response would leave the auction business to the austere rooms at Sotheby's. Today, eBay's market capitalization, at $15.5 billion, is more than one-third that of General Motors.

LESSON TWO

"All things that are, are with more
spirit chased than enjoyed."
—Gratiano, in *The Merchant of Venice*

Risk can best be analyzed and evaluated in light of the alternative options and its potential benefits in realizing a company's overall goals.

Portia evaluates and eventually selects Bassanio, not because he is ideal, but because he is better than her other options. And choosing him is consistent with her overall goals. While he has several entries on the debit side, Bassanio's major asset is that he fits into Portia's plan to acquire an accommodating husband. She puts the point nicely: "He is well paid that is well satisfied."

Antonio, coming within a hair of losing his life, never expresses regret for risking his pound of flesh since that conforms with his primary goal of helping Bassanio. Today's corporate executives should, of course, exercise better judgment than Antonio, but, like him, establish their goals before evaluating the options and making their choices. As in his case, personal relationships tend to cloud business judgment; one sure way to break up families and friendships is to go into business together.

As in Portia's case, risks run rampant in mergers and acquisitions, especially when the transaction is contested, like hers, by more than one eager suitor. Given Portia's assets, a wide range of wooers wish to become her husband. Having clearly established her goal, however, she knows who is and is not suitable.

This sensible approach is not always followed in today's big businesses. In January 1998, SmithKline Beecham and GlaxoWellcome suddenly announced a merger, but by the end of February they had called it off. As Gloucester says in *Henry VIII,* "Hasty marriage seldom proveth well." They simply couldn't agree on which key managers would lead the merged company. This is something they should have discussed and come to some kind of understanding about before announcing the change in status, much as Portia and Bassanio do. They both realize that she will be managing partner in the merged enterprise.

Not evaluating what is or isn't a good business fit can have serious repercussions. Circuit City failed to analyze such risks properly and consequently suffered. When its CEO, Richard Sharp, decided to jump-start the company's growth in 1993, he expanded the parent company's merchandise to encompass everything from small home appliances to secondhand cars. Because the company had built a highly trained sales force, he figured branching out would be a snap. Besides, the company extended credit to consumers, making it easy to expand his product line. Or so he said.

"His promises were, as he then was, mighty," says Katherine in *Henry VIII*, "but his performance, as he is now, nothing." The move has been worse than that. Car Max, the used-car lots in which Circuit City owns a 75 percent stake, lost $23.5 million on $1.5 billion in sales in 1998. Circuit City has decided not to expand beyond Car Max's thirty-one dealerships, whereas Sharp had previously pledged to open as many as ninety dealerships before 2002.

LESSON THREE

"The Devil can cite Scripture for his purpose."

—Antonio, in *The Merchant of Venice*

When it comes to making business decisions, what initially seems like hard fact and firm data often turns out to be something altogether more intangible. This is a particularly lethal circumstance for startups, which usually lack financial staying power.

Sometimes misreading occurs simply because executives wear all-too-human blinders. Other times it is because some businesspeople refuse to open their minds to options that they dismiss as unthinkable. For instance, when the aerospace industry plummeted in the early 1990s, most involved CEOs initially sought to hunker down and stay the course. In contrast, CEO and ex-astronaut William A. Anders offered the "unthinkable" idea that his company, General Dynamics, break up and sell off its pieces. After careful analysis, his board went along. The shareholders didn't have to think about the unthinkable for long before they started receiving rich returns.

While casting wide for facts by which to judge the options, corporate executives must be diligent but wary. For what seems like a hard fact one minute—the Venetian laws permitting Shylock to take the pound of flesh—can get trumped by other hard facts the next, such as other laws that punish "aliens" who spill Christian blood.

Moreover, hard facts can soon prove soft. It seemed

indisputable that the new person in the Venice court-room was a young male attorney from Padua, whereas actually she was a cunning female socialite from Belmont. Even Bassanio appreciates the danger of so-called facts as he speaks about "the seeming truth, which cunning times put on to entrap the wisest."

Yet more common in contemporary business is the absence of clear facts necessary to the decision-maker when having them counts most. In *Othello*, the Venetian authorities summon the Moor to repel a sneak Turkish invasion of Cyprus. The Duke is flustered by the conflicting intelligence reports coming in from his field commanders. One senator mentions that his reports "say one hundred seven galleys" of enemy ships; the Duke laments, "and mine one hundred forty;" while yet another senator adds to the confusion: "and mine two hundred."

Then a "messenger from the galleys" arrives, believing he is the first to break the news. Asked how many ships the Turks have under way, he answers with great precision and emphasis: "Of thirty sail."

Like many top executives facing a major decision, the Duke must grapple with alleged "facts" that are contradictory. In his case, investigating further won't help; there is neither time nor patience to find out the true number. The decision must be made promptly, as Othello is to be dispatched that very night to repel the invaders. Should he plan to face thirty or as many as two hundred enemy ships in the morning? After all, the actual number should make a huge difference in strategy and tactics.

Even in situations muddled by serious contradictions, an executive should keep in mind both the "known unknowns"—some number of Turkish ships are attacking Cyprus—and "unknown unknowns," or critical factors that cannot be anticipated—like weather conditions when the battle commences, or a new uprising far from Cyprus that may suddenly demand Othello's leadership.

Rarely do "known unknowns" prove fatal for companies, since their managements usually focus on them. Rather, it is the "unknown unknowns" that can, and often do, kill not only the balance sheet but also a senior manager's career.

Even established firms aren't always adept at anticipating or managing "unknown unknowns." In the summer of 1999, Coca-Cola, the world's number-one soft drink company, was lambasted for its failure to keep the public informed after dozens of people said they became sick after drinking Cokes in Belgium.

Only after massive criticism from consumer groups in France and Germany did chief executive and chairman M. Douglas Ivester issue an apology. The consumer groups merely wanted Coke's management to speak to them fairly, just as Hamlet asks of his players, "We'll have a speech straight. Come, give us a taste of your quality." Initially, however, all they received was Ivester's recitation of the company's history of providing first-rate products to its consumers. "One hundred thirteen years of our success has been based on the trust consumers have in that quality," he noted.

Yet Coca-Cola at first did little to inform consumers

of the problem, which made the company look heart-less as well as careless.

Lack of planning for managing risk was also evident at Foodmaker, the parent company of Jack-in-the-Box, which has only recently begun to recover financially from a food poisoning outbreak in 1993. To be sure, chief executive Robert Nugent began well after reports came in that the company's hamburger meat was conta-minated by E. coli bacteria, causing a number of con-sumers to fall sick. Foodmaker rapidly stopped selling hamburgers, recalled possibly contaminated meat from its distributors, got rid of the suppliers of the tainted meat, and began cooking food at higher temperatures. Nugent even agreed to take responsibility for medical expenses stemming from the contamination.

But the otherwise savvy CEO failed to handle cer-tain aspects of this risk adeptly. A week passed before Foodmaker publicly accepted blame for the fiasco. In the meantime, Nugent blamed the meat supplier and government health officials for failing to keep Food-maker informed on the state's newest food-safety guidelines.

After bringing in a new public-relations firm, the company tried to rebuild its image, but profits took a dive. Between 1993 and mid-1995, Foodmaker lost $167 million as sales dropped 18 percent. The company cut employee salaries and retooled its food-handling system.

However, as more stories of food poisoning linked to other companies were reported, the press often came back to Foodmaker with questions. This kept putting Foodmaker's mishap back in the headlines but it also gave Foodmaker an opportunity to show journalists the advances the company had made in food safety. Foodmaker also rebuilt its relationship with franchisees, to whom it had to pay $44 million in settling lawsuits after the poisoning scare.

Gradually the company rebounded. With 1998 sales at $1.2 billion and $67 million in net earnings, Foodmaker is opening more than one hundred Jack-in-the-Box restaurants in 1999.

LESSON FOUR

"It is a good divine that
follows his own instructions."
—Portia, in *The Merchant of Venice*

When finally approaching a big decision, even the most passionate of executives must act dispassionately. When with Bassanio, Portia takes herself aside to assure that her reason prevails over her emotions. She remarks to Nerissa about the dangers of being soft-hearted rather than hard-headed: "The brain may devise laws for the blood, but a hot temper leaps over a cold decree."

For business leaders, acting dispassionately is toughest when dealing with their own ideas, and they tend to support their own creations over those of others. One survey revealed that 58 percent of new product ideas conceived by the workforce failed, as opposed to 74 percent of those originating in senior management. (The best ideas usually come from the service, marketing, and sales departments since they know customers best.)

It is equally important to judge the ideas of others objectively. Comedienne Joan Rivers's jewelry retailing firm, JR Worldwide, now with an estimated $43 million in annual revenue, almost went broke a few years ago.

In the early nineties Rivers's previous jewelry company was so successful that Arthur Toll, the former CEO of Regal Communications Corp., persuaded her to sell it for $14 million worth of stock in his company. Rivers bit. Then, in 1994, Toll's firm went bankrupt and Rivers lost everything. It took years to rebuild her entrepreneurial holdings. In December 1998 Toll and one of his officers at Regal were charged with fraudulently inflating Regal's stock price in order to buy Rivers's firm. (Both have pleaded not guilty.) Rivers now says she'll never blindly trust anyone to advise her about her business again, whether or not that person claims to have more expertise than she does.

LESSON FIVE

"Men that hazard all do so in hope
of fair advantages."

—The Prince of Morocco,
in *The Merchant of Venice*

Executives who wager *all* usually do so foolishly. As Antonio teaches, companies had best avoid digging narrow but deep holes, wherein the risk may be remote but the consequences of failure are ruinous.

A severe case was the near collapse of Long Term Capital Management in 1998. The hedge fund was founded by a former vice-chairman of Salomon Brothers, a former vice-chairman of the Federal Reserve, two Nobel Laureates in economics, and more Ph.D.s per square foot than could be found in a Harvard faculty lounge. As Celia says in *As You Like It,* "The little foolery that wise men have makes a great show."

The disaster occurred because the group took on margin loans and other astronomically leveraged debt in order to bet on tiny anomalies in the market they thought were predictable. Investors, among them many major university endowments, gave them free rein, assuming their money was safe in the hands of such an accomplished assemblage. It turned out, however, that brilliance and good judgment may keep little company with each other.

For a while the fund grew so fast that its investment department couldn't keep up with the money pouring in. The managers actually had to kick people out of the fund. But, before long, the sudden devaluation of the Russian ruble destroyed the fund's very foundation—an expected decline in the differential between certain related interest rates. The astronomical leverage amassed previously sank its teeth into the fund's investors; they lost 40 percent of their capital in one month. This loss of equity caused the leverage to jump still further.

Consequently fourteen major banks and brokerage houses, fearful of losing what they had already lent, coughed up another $3.6 billion to try to keep the fund afloat. Ultimately many people lost a lot of real money on a "sure thing." The fund has now agreed to help investors cash out, but at a substantial loss compared to what they would have earned by randomly investing in the stock market. "Thus hath the candle singed the moth," Portia aptly summarizes this case study in precipitous action. "O, these deliberate fools! When they do choose, they have the wisdom by their wit to lose."

LESSON SIX

"You may as well do anything most

hard as seek to soften that."

—Antonio, in *The Merchant of Venice*

Risk must not only be taken but thereafter be managed.

Once a decision is reached on a risky proposition, executives must organize the team to "do anything most hard" to overcome impediments that arise. Otherwise they run the risk of finding themselves in Antonio's predicament, struggling to cope with a situation that has spun out of control. It is easy for small problems to mushroom through a steady stream of neglect.

It is appalling that neither Antonio, so successful a trader, nor the Duke, the CEO of Venice, even attempt any risk management.

Portia assumes the role of risk manager primarily because there is no alternative. In a corporation where choices do exist, one person should be assigned responsibility for overcoming each hurdle. That person should shine a bright spotlight on all known sources of risk. Once highlighted, these hot spots need to be addressed at once, measured regularly, and reported on periodically. This entails creating backup approaches, clear checkpoints, and milestone targets to hit before proceeding to the next phase. And it's prudent to have prearranged off-ramps if things *really* go wrong. The best risk managers assemble "red teams" of experienced hands, independent of responsibility for the project, who furnish reality checks at predetermined stages.

While risks must be scrupulously managed in any business endeavor, four special risks require most careful management in special circumstances.

First, executives handling *startups* should focus on business forecasts, the established competition's strength, barriers to entering the field, financing terms, market demand, cost control, and excessive costs. Unless startups are carefully managed, a "death spiral" begins when sales don't match projections while costs exceed them.

Second, *taking a company public* demands that management focus on the timing of the move and the adequacy of the capital raised.

Third, in *turnarounds,* the quality and discipline of leadership, especially in meeting commitments, should be management's top focus. Managers in these situations should accept no boundary conditions, such as employees claiming, "That's the way we've always done it around here." That way obviously landed the companies in big trouble in the first place.

Fourth, for established and bloated companies, executives should focus on *divestitures.* If a business line does not fit or perform, it should be sold—fast. Otherwise it remains a distraction to those managing risks in the core business. Besides, it may be worth more to another company, especially if the timing of the divestiture is right. "For I must tell you friendly in your ear," Rosalind tells Phebe in *As You Like It.* "Sell when you can. You are not for all markets."

One of the best risk managers to work a big problem in a most difficult situation was Bill LeMessurier. His dilemma was sky-high.

LeMessurier, a highly regarded executive and engineer, was responsible for the structural design of New York's Citicorp Building at 53rd Street and Lexington Avenue. After his building had been completed in 1977 and was fully occupied, LeMessurier received a telephone call from a student claiming that his professor considered the building to be unsafe. LeMessurier patiently explained the basis of his design and thanked the student for the call.

But, like the best executives everywhere, he looked into the information he had received and determined that a series of events in the design process had combined to collectively weaken the structure. He concluded that the skyscraper could, indeed, collapse in the type of windstorm that blew into New York once every sixteen years or so.

Since no one else knew of this problem—especially not the thousands of people working in the building— he faced a distinctly non-career-enhancing situation, as well as a moral dilemma.

LeMessurier took the right and bold approach. He set out to alert others to the danger and sought to find a way to solve the problem without wrecking the entire structure. LeMessurier started at the top, asking to see the chairman of Citicorp, but he couldn't get past the palace guard. Next, he tried the president's office but found a moat around that castle, too.

Persistent, he called on John Reed, then executive vice president of Citicorp, who listened calmly and carefully. Reed didn't panic; indeed, he didn't even call his lawyers. Instead he and LeMessurier began their risk-management duties by calling in the building's architect and devising a solution. They fervently hoped that new structural reinforcements could be completed before any big storm hit New York but formulated an evacuation plan in case of such an event. Engineers began the modifications on an expedited basis. Fortunately the changes needed were not excessive, and before long the reinforced building was declared safe.

Luck, which so often intercedes on Shakespeare's stage, rewarded LeMessurier and his colleagues for their honesty and diligence. When Hurricane Ella was headed on a collision course for New York before the repairs were completed, it turned back to sea at the last minute. Not only that, the New York newspapers were hit by a strike the day after the public announcement of the problem.

E. Rachel Hubka also understands the need to manage and not just accept risks. Her firm, Rachel's Bus Co., hires part-time workers that other firms avoid. Believing, like Marcius says in *Coriolanus*, that "the gods sent not corn for the rich men only," her company hires the unemployed from Chicago's inner city, including some on welfare. Hubka's company, based in North Lawndale, Illinois, hires many part-time bus drivers, and she wishes to open up opportunities to a neglected sector of the population.

But Hubka hasn't gone into this risky business naively. She understands that people who have been out of the workforce may need training and other help. She offers an initial twenty-hour training program, covering everything from driving techniques to handling disruptive students, and a twenty-hour refresher class every year. The company also works with a local school to enable employees to prepare for high-school equivalency diplomas and learn computer skills.

The arrangement pays off for Hubka, whose small, ten-year-old firm brings in $5 million a year.

As every executive must know, the consequence of failing to manage risk can be dire. Consider: One day in October 1997, the share price of Oxford Health Plans plunged from $68.75 to $25.75, when Oxford revealed that its earnings had been crimped by computer problems that messed up its payment and billing systems. The HMO, which had enjoyed a period of rapid growth, had neglected to deal with this problem until it created a disaster. It took Oxford months to sort through the myriad of difficulties. By August 1998, its share price reached a nadir of $6.

Oxford has begun a turnaround by trying to actively manage risk. It is withdrawing from unprofitable markets, reducing the number of its employees, consolidating its office space, and taking other cost-saving measures. At this time, however, Oxford's fate remains unclear.

Much of risk management is more of an art than a science. Those special but somewhat ethereal attributes, creativity and judgment, count for a lot. Many an executive has discovered that doing the right thing is even tougher than knowing the right thing to do. As Portia admits, "I can easier teach twenty what were good to be done, than to be one of the twenty to follow mine own teaching."

ACT V

CRISIS MANAGEMENT
"Confusion Hath Made Its Masterpiece"

[DRAMATIS EXECUTIVUS SUMMARIUS]

As on the stage, some crises in business slink in quietly while others burst explosively. Regardless of origin, their consequences can be as catastrophic to a business as they are to a kingdom, and as disastrous to a businessperson as they are to a king. Crises become confusing in themselves and add to the confusion around them, as Macduff comments in the quote above from *Macbeth*.

From its opening moments of uncertainty to its body-strewn last scene, *Hamlet* is rife with crises. As it turns out, the play's eponymous hero, Hamlet, is far from being a model crisis manager. While the drama's originating crisis—the ghost's command that he avenge his father's murder—revolves around him, Hamlet fails to take control and *act*. Rather, he struggles and reacts.

Hamlet, in fact, is a case study on how *not* to handle a crisis. While this is instructive up to a point, it has limited impact since there are an infinite variety of ways to fail but only a few ways to succeed. Besides, Hamlet's crisis is personal. Even though the outcome affects others, the abstract and reflective Prince deals with his predicament almost entirely by himself—when he deals with it at all.

In contrast, Claudius, his despised uncle and stepfather, makes more of a success of it. The focused, operation-driven ruler handles his crises well by acting boldly. He explicitly appoints a crisis team and decides who is to run it (*he* is). Devising a tight action plan with backups and seizing opportunities as they arise, he constantly keeps his stakeholders (his wife and subjects) clearly in mind. Candid and insightful, he consults outside experts as necessary. Most of all, he thinks creatively.

His actions offer the blueprint for every executive who faces a complicated unfolding crisis.

PROLOGUE

From the moment the drama opens, Elsinore swirls in crisis that doesn't stop until the final act. From the opening words "Who's there?" the play begins on an immediate note of fear. "Nay, answer me," snaps back the other night sentry, who then demands, "stand and unfold yourself." After the two guards greet each other, one confesses that he is "sick at heart," not exactly a sentiment common among Danish warriors.

This, probably Shakespeare's greatest play, contains more emotional reversals than any other. "O Gertrude, Gertrude," Claudius says woefully to his wife at one point, "when sorrows come, they come not as single spies but in battalions!"

Claudius is being characteristically conservative. Here sorrows arrive in divisions and are in fact instigated by Claudius himself. He commits a terrible crime, poisoning his brother, which he admits has "the primal eldest curse upon it." Claudius is steeped even deeper in sin than Cain since he's guilty of both fratricide *and* regicide. As if that's not enough, he marries his victim's widow, Queen Gertrude. Thus, Claudius's throne and marriage, both gained by crime, are illegitimate.

Nonetheless, Claudius shows impressive executive talents. With deft statesmanship, he uses diplomacy to stop a Norwegian invasion of Denmark without war. And, although fresh in office, Claudius controls his representatives tightly. When handing two envoys his written instructions, Claudius explicitly gives them "no further personal power more than the scope of these dilated articles allow." Though something of a control freak, Claudius knows how to handle dicey professional situations adeptly.

He tries to do the same in his personal life. Besides adjusting to his new roles as king and husband, he's also just become a stepfather, an awkward position in any case but much more so in this tense situation. As it often happens, it is the child's deportment toward the newcomer that is the problem and not the reverse.

While Claudius has committed murder, he, at least, feels terrible about it. He's no Richard III, who relishes evil. Indeed, he suffers from his actions. In an important aside to himself relatively early in the drama, Claudius says that thinking about "my deed" is horrendous, and ends with something of a primal shriek: "O heavy burden!"

Hamlet, in contrast, also kills people—the courtier Polonius, as well as his boyhood friends Rosencrantz and Guildenstern, Laertes, and, at long last, Claudius— but feels no sympathy for any of them. Both Hamlet and Claudius are also typical Shakespearean characters, that is, flawed humans, in all their contradictions. "The web of" all lives, as Lord Dumaine says in *All's Well That Ends Well*, "is of a mingled yarn, good and ill together." We learn of Claudius's "ill" character right away, but watch his "good" crisis management as he's faced with handling two of the gravest crises imaginable—the threat of death by Hamlet's hand and actual rebellion by Laertes, Polonius's son.

SCENE I

[Enter the King, looking regal but worried.]

Claudius's first crisis hits him hard in the "honeymoon period" of his personal and professional lives. The King, like most busy executives, does not see it coming.

While he may have legitimately expected a crisis from

his stepson Hamlet, he does not anticipate how the eccentric Prince will behave after his father's death. Everyone can see that Hamlet is beginning to act wild, yet the King takes no steps to confine him. What he does do is to permit Polonius, his key aide, to spy on his wife in her bedroom when she wishes to have a heart-to-heart talk with her troubled son. When they get under way, Hamlet stabs Polonius, who is hiding behind the curtain in his mother's bedroom.

Killing the old man doesn't stop Hamlet or even slow him down. He proceeds to talk to his mother— literally over Polonius' dead body—about her marriage in general and her sex life in particular.

Claudius learns of Polonius's killing from Gertrude. For an instant, he reacts like a sensitive man of the 1600s, sighing "O heavy deed!" Snapping out of it, he immediately gets the big picture, commenting, "It had been so with us, had we been there."

A fast-breaking crisis demands immediate and extreme action. Claudius acts decisively as he lays the necessary groundwork to Gertrude, to get rid of Hamlet, pointing out that "his liberty is full of threats to all—to you yourself, to us, to every one." Having addressed his main constituency, Claudius next thinks about his subjects.

Like any first-class executive, he has an instinctive grasp of public reaction. This is even more important in today's world of instant communications than in Claudius's Denmark. Nonetheless, he calculates "how dangerous is it that this man goes loose" and weighs popular perceptions. He understands that "yet must not we put the strong law on" Hamlet because "he's loved of the distracted multitude." For these valid reasons, "sudden sending [Hamlet] away must *seem* deliberate" —in other words, unhurried—even when it's not. Claudius is well aware that people will initially blame him—"It will be laid to us." As the kingdom's ruler, he should have kept "short, restrained, and out of haunt this mad young man."

Despite his grave public-relations woes, Claudius knows he can resolve a serious problem by using bad news to make some good moves. In short, he will send Hamlet to England and ask the English king to kill him.

Claudius then asks, "Where is he gone?" Gertrude replies, to "draw apart the body he hath kill'd." Claudius knows what to do, declaring, "The sun no sooner shall the mountains touch but we will ship him hence." He orders Rosencrantz and Guildenstern to find Hamlet at once and discover what he has done with the body. As in many modern management crises, the conclusion is reached quickly that something must be done.

At this stage, Claudius has no idea of the specific outcome of Polonius's murder but he knows it won't be good. To prepare, he consults with Gertrude, his partner in crisis management, and stresses that they must brace themselves, mentally and emotionally, for all that will befall them. Whatever it may bring, the new crisis will demand "all our majesty and skill" to handle. One of the most important things an executive can do, particularly in trying times, is to think positively. The least inkling of weakness and uncertainty will be magnified a thousand times over in the eyes of followers.

Then Claudius takes another necessary crisis-management step. Instinctively he understands the need for outside consultation. "Come, Gertrude," he says. "We'll call up our wisest friends and let them know both what we mean to do and what's untimely done." They can give advice and help plug damaging rumors.

Planning, questioning, giving clear and crisp orders, anticipating public reactions, seeking outside counsel—Claudius has his bases covered. Then, when he's about to resolve the threat of the unstable young Hamlet, Claudius comes face-to-face with his stepson and almost loses everything.

Scene II

[Enter a youngster, frolicking in the castle passageway, clothes disheveled and bloody.]

After Claudius orders Rosencrantz and Guildenstern to find Polonius's body, he orders Hamlet brought before him. "Now, Hamlet, where's Polonius?" he demands.

"At supper," is the wise-guy reply. "Not where he eats, but where he is eaten. But indeed, if you find him not within this month, you shall nose him as you go up the stair, into the lobby." After the King tells the guards, "Go seek him there," Hamlet makes another mockery, "He will stay till ye come."

The King duplicitously tells Hamlet, "This deed, for thine especial safety—which we do tender as we dearly grieve for that which thou hast done—must send thee hence with fiery quickness." Claudius orders the guards to take him "with speed aboard. Delay it not; I'll have him hence to-night."

At this point, the King must feel relief. Crisis Number 1—handling the avenging son—seems to be solved. Hamlet is about to be permanently removed from the family portrait.

But, even as Hamlet leaves, a new crisis, borne from the one managed successfully (thus far), looms large. The new crisis will take unexpected and strange twists and turns.

SCENE III

[Enter young woman, disheveled, holding flowers.]

Polonius's daughter Ophelia wanders in and about. As Hamlet's lover, she had worried about his going mad. Now, with her father killed by Hamlet's hand, *she* has gone mad. It often takes a crisis to determine which employees will come apart under pressure.

Gertrude and Claudius, aghast, watch and try to cope. Claudius tries to make some sense of what's happening by reviewing the crisis: "First, her father slain. Next, your son gone"—carefully explaining that it's not *his* doing—"he most violent author of his own just remove." And now the problem here with Ophelia. Claudius has a deft feel for people and astutely assesses the young girl's malady as schizophrenia: "Poor Ophelia divided from herself and her fair-judgment, without the which we are pictures or mere beasts."

Despite his insight into Ophelia's condition, he does not foresee the magnitude of the effect of Polonius's murder on his two children. Still, as a skilled crisis manager, Claudius anticipates that serious problems will stem from Laertes.

"Her brother is in secret come from France," he announces. In the midst of a crisis, information is absolutely essential, and somehow Claudius has gathered it. Laertes may have tried to return "in secret," but the King's intelligence-gathering network has picked up his whereabouts.

The outraged Laertes soon bursts into Elsinore leading a mob shouting, "Choose we! Laertes shall be king!" Claudius stays focused on events even as the mob, led by the agitated and angry Laertes, confronts him. Now that crisis has hit its zenith, the management team must gather every ounce of courage, decisiveness, judgment, and persuasion to handle it.

Laertes, who naively insists that the mob leave the throne room, thereby lessening his power just when he needs it most, is disrespectful and threatening. "O thou vile king, give me my father!" he demands.

Claudius, like every great crisis manager, attempts to stop the fighting and start the talking. "What is the cause, Laertes, that thy rebellion looks so giantlike?" he asks. "Why thou art thus incensed?"

Laertes repeats, "Where is my father?" In response, Claudius gets the facts out quickly. "Dead," he replies, and Claudius smoothly point outs, that "I am guiltless of your father's death, and am most sensibly in grief for it." The moment of maximum danger has passed, only to have another crisis erupt as the disheveled Ophelia enters again and her distraught brother utters, "Do you see this, O God?"

The pathetic young woman is a sad spectacle. Though Claudius customarily uses the "royal we," he shows Laertes that he feels his pain by resorting to first person, telling him, "I must commune with your grief, or you deny me right."

Thus does Claudius convey the fact that he cares, which is the first half of the essential message from a top leader in any crisis. The other half—"And I'm doing something about it right now"—comes a moment later.

He offers Laertes one crisis management principle he has already practiced, namely to seek outside counsel. He advises him, "Go but apart. Make choice of whom your wisest friends you will, and they shall hear and judge."

Claudius, as ever keen to control the situation, also offers Laertes a deal with built-in dividends for himself. If accepted, it can transform Claudius's main *problem* now—a major rebellion—into part of his ultimate *solution* of ending any threat from Hamlet in the future. (The Prince, recall, has been sent off to England to be killed, but Claudius can't be sure what will happen. Like any careful crisis manager, he has backup plans.)

The deal, as it must be in such a situation, is simple: either Claudius will abdicate or Laertes will submit to him. If Laertes finds that Claudius, "by direct or by collateral hand," was responsible for Polonius's death, then "we will our kingdom give, our crown, our life, and all that we call ours, to you in satisfaction."

Yet if no royal responsibility is found, Claudius asks him to "be you content to lend your patience to us, and we shall jointly labor" to avenge that death.

Laertes readily agrees, stating, "Let this be so." Claudius asks for Laertes's trust and explains that the murder was Hamlet's doing. When Laertes asks why "you proceeded not against these" clear crimes, the King answers directly. Once again, as an increasingly experienced crisis manager, he is the model of getting the truth out clearly and quickly.

"O, for two special reasons," he tells him. "The Queen his mother lives almost by [Hamlet's] looks," and she in turn is "so conjunctive to my life and soul" that Claudius must consider her desires.

After this personal consideration, political factors play a role: the public adores Hamlet. Putting Hamlet on trial or punishing him would only ricochet against the King.

Laertes, through Claudius's fine management skills, has now been incorporated into the King's team. No longer is he a part of the problem; he has now become a crucial part of the solution.

A messenger enters with a letter containing more bad news. Hamlet is back! He jumped off his ship onto a pirate vessel, and on arrival in England, ordered the murder of Rosencrantz and Guildenstern. Claudius learns an important management lesson: sending a problem employee to another division only creates problems in the new location.

Now the first crisis has returned in full force. Fortunately the King can use the fruits of his skillful handling of the second crisis (initiated by Laertes) to help him solve his first (initiated by Hamlet). Business crises have a way of boomeranging, too.

Before launching his project, though, he must tidy up the management structure. Just as there must be one public spokesman during a crisis, so must there be only one overall strategist and leader. As another superb royal crisis manager, Prince Hal, says in *Henry IV, Part I*, "Two stars keep not their motion in one sphere."

Claudius has decided that he will be that star. Having already turned Laertes from rebel to ally, Claudius now clarifies the reporting lines, an essential strategy for successful crisis management. He inquires, "Will you be ruled by me?" Laertes responds, "Ay, my lord" just "so you will not overrule me to a peace" by surrender.

What ensues is another of Shakespeare's magnificent depictions of a successful business meeting. It is well organized, well paced, creative in its planning, clear in its outcome, and involves only those who have a contribution to make or a responsibility to carry out.

Now in the chair, literally and figuratively, Claudius sets the goal: Hamlet must be killed, but in such a way that no blame can be attributed to either of the plotters. They must decide the means "under the which he shall not choose but fall; and for his death no wind but even his mother shall uncharge the practice and call it accident."

Laertes signs on and volunteers to do whatever the King devises. "It falls right," states Claudius, who has now established himself as CEO and relegated Laertes to COO. To formulate the master plan, the King begins to brainstorm by musing about Laertes's reputation as a fine swordsman and recalls Hamlet's envy of his skill.

He then engages in risk management by reinforcing Laertes's commitment to the overall mission. Claudius has observed firsthand that the young man can be hot-headed one minute and compliant the next. The likelihood of Laertes telling others of Claudius's intention to kill Hamlet may be very small, but the consequences of such a revelation would be catastrophic. If that happened, the King would surely lose his wife and probably his crown.

Having calculated all this, Claudius makes a maximum effort to reduce risk and motivate his one-man workforce. He dramatically alters the tone and topic of the meeting. Formerly cozy and chatty, it now becomes taunting and confrontational. He poses a radically different question to the lad. "Laertes, was your father dear to you?"

Before Laertes has time to recover, Claudius hurls another assault: "Or are you like the painting of a sorrow, a face without a heart?"

Laertes says, offended, "Why ask you this?"

Seeking total commitment, Claudius slyly challenges, "What would you undertake to show yourself your father's son in deed, more than in words?" Laertes wastes no words: "To cut his throat in the church!" That will do. Now Claudius presents the strategy. Like any good plan, it's not too intricate. Together they'll praise Laertes's swordsmanship, wager he can whip Hamlet, and sneak in an unblunted sword by which Laertes will kill him, seemingly by accident.

Laertes, delighted, agrees, and then suggests a backup plan. He'll anoint his sword with deadly poison. Claudius deems the stakes high enough to warrant not one but *two* backup systems: The last fail-safe system is a poisoned chalice.

Just when it seems that all is finally under control, the Queen arrives and breaks terrible news, telling Laertes, "Your sister's drowned." Crises tend to be amoebalike, spontaneously reproducing themselves.

Laertes, overwhelmed, rushes out. Riveted on this new crisis, Claudius says nothing about Ophelia and focuses instead on the possiblity of Laertes's again becoming a threat. "How much I had to do to calm his rage," he tells Gertrude. "Now fear I this will give it start again. Therefore let's follow."

One crisis, at least, is handled, and a clear and attainable plan to end the other is in place. Claudius has proven himself most royal as crisis manager.

ACTING LESSONS

While Claudius's crimes are deplorable, with their own version of poison pills, shark watches, and bear hugs, there is still much to be learned from his crisis-management skills. By observing his handling of a series of connected problems, today's corporate executives can learn ten lessons on how to act when a crisis hits.

LESSON ONE

"This bodes some strange eruption to our state."

—Horatio, in *Hamlet*

Executives must both expect crisis and prepare for one that hits hard, and soon. "The readiness is all," says Hamlet, a lesson he learns late and implements poorly.

Claudius could not know that Hamlet would discover that he had killed his father, or that Hamlet would kill Polonius. Yet, as soon as each happens, his instincts tell him to expect a crisis. From that time on, he thinks proactively, before the precise contours of the crisis become clear.

Claudius dispatches Hamlet at the first opportunity, and he skillfully defuses Laertes's rebellion. While keeping his cool, he handles a potential p.r. nightmare, and creatively formulates effective strategies for each crisis.

Executives who prepare for crises can cope much better than those who wait for bad surprises. Cassius, for one, understood the value of anticipating problems. "Since the affairs of men rest still incertain, let's reason with the worst that may befall," he says as he prepares to go into battle.

One of the few organizations created specifically to deal with crises, the American Red Cross constantly prepares for disasters. As its former president Elizabeth Dole has said, "The middle of a disaster is the poorest possible time to establish new relationships and to introduce ourselves to new organizations. When you have taken the time to build rapport, then you can make a call at two a.m. when the river's rising and expect to launch a well-planned, smoothly conducted response."

Likewise, the shrewdest business leaders realize that it's important to be prepared for whatever crises their venture may bring, whether caused by rogue employees, implementation and system failures, technological obsolescence, tainted products, accidents, or labor disputes.

At the same time, executives face heavy pressure

to produce quarterly profits, particularly in publicly held companies, which, on average, undergo ownership turnovers every two years. Consequently they don't take time or make the effort to plan for disasters. They are so pressed by immediate problems that they relegate theoretical problems—even those that could prove catastrophic to their firms—to the "do someday" pile. Many share the sentiment Henry Kissinger expressed when he was secretary of state: "Next week there can't be any crisis. My schedule's already full." Some business leaders simply demote crisis planning to the type of unnecessary work Gratiano describes in *The Merchant of Venice* as "mending of highways in summer, where the ways are fair enough."

In fact, a Fortune 500 survey found that 89 percent of CEOs considered business crises as inevitable as death and taxes, yet half lacked any crisis plans. This means that they must cope with disasters that could have been headed off when still more manageable as mere problems. Moreover, they get into the uncomfortable position of having to wing it, not for better but for worse, when a crisis does hit.

To prepare for a crisis, prudent executives should draw up a "worry list" of (1) five or at most ten events that can most easily and gravely land the business in a crisis, (2) a brief summary of the consequences of each such scenario, (3) the cost of prevention, and (4) the likelihood of occurrence. Such anticipated events can often be managed before the problem balloons into a crisis. As Clarence says in *Henry VI, Part III,* "A little fire is quickly trodden out which, being suffered, rivers cannot quench."

King Richard II, unlike Claudius, lacks the character to cope with crises since he is convinced that he was chosen by God to hold the throne. Such an executive is at least halfway to making *Fortune*'s list of failed CEOs. As a rebellion grows, he acknowledges the problem but does nothing about it since he believes he is invincible. "If angels fight, weak men must fall, for Heaven still guards the right," he declares.

Then Richard resorts to something even more ephemeral than those noncombat angels: "Is not the King's name twenty thousand names?" he asks. Still unable to absorb the fact that a real crisis has hit, Richard finds himself "all dissolved to tears." Before long he's off the throne and into jail, where he'll be killed.

The brokerage industry is full of executives who deemed themselves to be "divine-right rulers" in their own realms. When a few small startup companies started offering cheap online trading to consumers in the early eighties, old-line, full-service brokerages barely noticed. They had little incentive, as they were happy to collect $100 per trade from customers who sought the advice of their brokers.

But these customers weren't as loyal as the brokerages thought—or, at least, they were less loyal to their money managers than to their money. Lower trading fees saved money that could be invested in the booming stock market, so rather than fight, they switched. Online brokerage firms like Ameritrade and Etrade raced to be first to lure these thrifty customers away from the traditional brokerages. "Fruits that blossom first," Iago tells us in *Othello*, "will first be ripe."

Before long, that blossom became hard to ignore. Charles Schwab & Co. was one of the first large discount houses to jump on the new trend. Executives there realized early that they had better offer e-trading before they experienced one of the most common business crises: vanishing customers.

As a consequence they introduced trading stock online in 1995. Although the $29.95 trades it offers cost more than the five-dollar or eight-dollar trades of online discounters, Schwab has managed to attract an increasing number of online traders with a combination of its low-cost fees and convenience. Its online trade customers jumped from 1.2 million people at the end of 1997 to 1.8 million by June 30, 1998.

Forrester Research, an independent research firm that studies technological change, estimates that by 2003, 9.7 million households will manage their assets in online brokerage accounts, up from less than 4 million households in early 1999.

As a result of successes like these, other firms are now joining up. Prudential Securities, A. G. Edwards & Sons, and Tucker Anthony are currently looking to offer some kind of online trading. In June 1999, Merrill Lynch announced the launch of its own Internet brokerage operation. The question is whether these companies, like Richard II, waited too long to stop the threat of rebels to their realm.

Even when the initial crisis is under control, it's important to anticipate secondary effects. King Lear never imagines that banishing Cordelia could lead to his ruin and the destruction of his country. Antony never considers that Cleopatra could betray him during the great naval battle at Actium, which leads him to suicide. Neither Brutus nor Cassius conceive that their assassination of Caesar could trigger a civil war. Nonetheless, all of these life-altering, and empire-altering, events come to pass.

In business, the same applies. When Hurricane Andrew devastated south Florida in 1992, local telephone companies knew they would face a major shortage of telephone poles, wires, and switches, but never imagined what would be one of their biggest problems in solving the crisis. What flummoxed them was that local daycare centers, upon whom many of the phone companies' field operators depended, had shut down because of storm damage. Thus the workers most needed to restore the state's telecommunications systems were forced to stay home to care for their children. Eventually the companies found retirees, who, as the Duchess in *Richard II* says, "hath love in thy old blood [of] living fire" to run the centers so their employees could come to work.

LESSON TWO

"There is nothing either good or bad
but thinking makes it so."

—Hamlet

When managing a crisis, it is essential that executives pay close attention to whether customers think something is "good" or "bad" and not just to the technical aspects of the situation.

As Shakespeare observes through a character aptly named Rumour in *Henry IV, Part II*, rumors are "a pipe blown by surmises, jealousies, conjectures, and of so easy and so plain a stop that the blunt monster with uncounted heads, the still-discordant wavering multitude, can play upon it." He goes on to say that "rumour's tongues are worse than true wrongs."

When a crisis starts erupts, rumors start to fly. This holds especially true in our Matt Drudge era, when the Internet turns a rumor into "a feather for each wind that blows," as Leontes says in *The Winter's Tale*. This rumormongering can do major damage to even the most solidly run company, and do it at fiberoptic speed.

The leaders of Quigley Corp., which makes Cold-Eeze zinc lozenges, learned that the ruinous effects of "rumour's tongue" are magnified on the Internet. In 1996 after scientific research showed that its product offered among the best relief available for the common cold, the share price of their stock shot from $1 to $37. Cold-Eeze was featured on programs like *60 Minutes* and became so popular that customers lined up at stores to buy it.

Then someone started a rumor campaign against the company. The accusations bring to mind Bassanio's humorous description in *The Merchant of Venice* of a man whose "reasons are as two grains of wheat hid in two bushels of chaff. You shall seek all day ere you find them, and when you have them they are not worth the search."

The "reasons," however, became worth the search since they damaged the company so severely. Among other things, they alleged that the company had ties to the mob.

In late 1996, an impostor pretending to be company chairman Guy Quigley slipped onto the company's Web site and conducted a chat in which he blamed the decline of the stock on disorganization in the company and other problems. Industry analysts suspected that the culprits were stock shorters—investors who bet that a company's stock will go down. The scammers used anonymous remailer sites so their messages couldn't be traced.

Whoever they were, the company stock steadily plummeted. Currently it is trading at under $6 a share. "The Internet is a killing zone," remarked Charles Phillips, the company's COO, who may have been feeling the pain of Titus Andronicus: "These words are razors to my wounded heart."

The risk of poisonous rumors has grown so great that companies should take aggressive preventive measures well before a crisis comes. The model was established by Kaiser Permanente, the California-based HMO, which set up an internal Web forum called Rumor Check. Employees can raise complaints and questions, including those that recycle cyber rumors about corporate policies and practices. These are monitored by Bob Hughes, a public-relations consultant for the firm, who uses this technique to clarify the HMO's position on labor issues and stop false rumors about mergers and potential takeovers.

In the Web era, it's a huge mistake to underestimate the speed at which rumors may travel on the Web and how damaging they may be. "Rumors fly," says Jim Horton, a senior director at Robert Marston & Associates. His public-relations firm in New York City has worked with many clients on handling crises. He says, "There is probably no faster rumormongering tool in the world today."

If just two or three disgruntled customers, dealers for the company's products, or employees of a rival firm put up a Web site complaining about a company's products, they can deliver what Hamlet called a "rhapsody of words" to create the impression that there is a groundswell of dissatisfaction.

Sometimes, however, such individuals raise legitimate concerns. Other times, creators of complaint sites may simply be hotheads. Often their points are, as King Richard III says, "too shallow and too quick." But they can nonetheless be effective. If the information they post makes its way into newsgroups and the general media gets wind of it, a company may find itself with a very damaging untrue story to rebut.

Today's companies now have their public-relations staff monitor the Web daily for misinformation so they can stanch rumors. By studying what is posted, they may discover—as Horton's firm did once when representing a computer company—that the ringleaders behind a seeming groundswell of negative rumors are only a handful of people. By offering a solution to their complaint, or even an explanation, the rumor can be stopped as fast as it starts.

"In a crisis," says Horton, "facts count." Managements most adept at public relations and crisis prevention (or, if necessary, crisis management) will get the facts on their Web site without referencing those who are circulating the damaging information. One strategy is to post a list of frequently asked questions (FAQ). Whatever they do, their message must be scrupulously accurate. In the world of rumor control, credibility is everything.

At the same time, the traditional media shouldn't be ignored. "When you think about a business crisis, you want people to have one interpretation and one interpretation only," says Al Rothstein, who specializes in crisis management. "That's one advantage the Web has over traditional media. When you talk to a reporter or a broadcast journalist, what you say can be edited."

(If Claudius had the wherewithal to follow our advice and put up a crisis Web page, he could have controlled his crisis even better.)

LESSON THREE

"The time is out of joint, O cursed spite,
that ever I was born to set it right."

—Hamlet

Even before a crisis breaks, it's important to select members of the crisis-management team. When crises come to Claudius, he turns to Gertrude and Polonius, and uses Rosencrantz and Guildenstern. He knows it is important to pull together a team to handle the crisis rationally.

Companies in crisis should keep their crisis team small. It should be headed by the CEO and include at least one lawyer, the designated spokesperson, an out-side advisor to offer an independent view, and insiders who know the situation best. The crisis team leader must make the final call on all major decisions. "How in one house should many people under two commands hold amity?" Regan asks in *King Lear*. "'Tis hard, almost impossible."

When John Ryan III, chief executive of Mine Safety Appliances Co., learned that one of the company's compressed-air cylinders had exploded at a fire station in Detroit in 1995, he put together a small crisis team and traveled to the scene.

The device in question helps firefighters breathe dur-ing fires; if others exploded, people could be killed. To prevent this, Ryan told distributors and firefighters not to use the cylinders and informed the news media about the problem. The team also posted messages on Web sites that firefighters were likely to see, warning them to retire the cylinders from use, at least temporarily.

As it later turned out, the cylinder had exploded because it had been run over by a fire truck and damaged. But the company, while suffering short-term losses, greatly enhanced its long-term public image. Even more important, the crisis team headed off the possibility of fatalites caused by the use of its product.

After this episode Ryan, like all good executives, moved beyond the crisis without bitterness and got back to business. As the Duke says in *Othello*: "To mourn a mischief that is past and gone is the next way to draw new mischief on."

LESSON FOUR

"Report me and my cause aright to the unsatisfied."

—Hamlet

In a crisis, informing the public promptly with all available and legally disclosable information is invariably the right course to follow. The single fully informed crisis spokesperson must relate all the known facts as well as the actions that have been, and will be, taken. The goal is to get it right, get it quick, get it out, and get it over. No crisis improves with age.

When Laertes and his mob rush into Elsinore, Claudius doesn't hide. Rather, he stands, unwavering, at the door to receive them. This sends the crowd the powerful message that he both cares about the situation and will get control of it. Meticulously analyzing public perception, Claudius addresses it at once.

The failure to be up-front shook the rock-solid Intel Corporation in 1994. After a college professor discovered that his Pentium microprocessor chip had trouble performing complex mathematical calculations precisely, the professor thoughtfully contacted Intel to report the anomaly.

Intel treated the problem as a purely technical issue instead of a potential public-relations nightmare, and gave this well-meaning truth-sayer a polite brush-off. When the professor went online to see if others also had this problem, many messages came flooding back. Ironically, when the company belatedly offered to replace the chip free, hardly anyone accepted. Only 1 to 3 percent of individual consumers, who constituted two-thirds of the buyers of computers containing Pentium chips, even bothered to respond. People didn't want a new chip; they wanted to *know* that they could get a new chip if they wanted one. The company reportedly took a $475 million charge against earnings, the cost of being less than straightforward with its customers. Still, Intel eventually learned from its callous view and corrected its stand.

In contrast, a forthright approach saved the Odwalla Juice company from going under. In 1996 potentially deadly *E. coli* bacteria were found in its organic juice products. Sixty-one people fell ill, and, tragically, one child died. The company president, Greg Steltenpohl, knew that the small firm in Half Moon Bay, California, could soon face a dire fate itself if he did not handle this disaster effectively.

Like most companies, Odwalla had no well-developed crisis communications plan in place. Yet, Steltenpohl intuited the need to drop everything, following Lepidus's counsel cited earlier from *Antony and Cleopatra:* "Small matters to greater matters must give way."

Twenty minutes after learning of the contamination, Odwalla held a press conference to announce that it was recalling all its products containing unpasteurized apple juice, the culprit in this case. But, as the bad news spread, Steltenpohl realized that wasn't enough. The newly formed crisis-management team decided to use the Internet to reach the public. It flew in Matthew Harrington, a public-relations expert from Edelman Public Relations in San Francisco, to create a crisis Web site. The savvy publicity firm had already reserved a Web site for potential crisis communications by its clients. By late afternoon the same day, they had posted a letter to the public on the Web site that explained what they were doing to ensure that their consumers were safe.

The Odwalla Web site answered customers' fears and concerns in a straightforward manner. As Brutus says in *Julius Caesar,* "There are no tricks in plain and simple faith." Because executives at the firm lacked expertise with illnesses related to *E. coli* or its treatment, they established links to other health-related Web sites where worried customers could look up information. Within the first forty-eight hours, the makeshift site had twenty thousand hits.

After six consecutive quarters of losses sparked by the bacteria scare, the company finally turned the corner and reported a profit in the fiscal year ending in 1998. It was able to boost its sales to $59 million, close to precrisis levels. (Revenues had declined from $59 million to $52.6 million in 1997.) This year, the growth is continuing. Third-quarter net sales in 1999 were up to $19.1 million, compared to $15.4 million the same quarter last year.

LESSON FIVE

"Bring me to the test."

—Hamlet

Today's executives should designate a crisis center and furnish it so the crisis team can construct a strategy, coordinate necessary activities, and get their message out to the people who need to hear it.

For Claudius, the castle of Elsinore is the natural crisis center. Contained and guarded, its messengers are ready to run at a moment's notice.

For corporate leaders, the crisis center should be located in the headquarters near the CEO's office and be equipped with both a backup computer system in a different geographical area and reliable communications equipment, as well as lists of phone numbers, e-mail and street addresses of key customers, suppliers, community services, employees, shareholders, and outside partners such as law firms and banks. As some businesses have learned the hard way, lists of key suppliers, clients, and other important people should also be stored off the premises, in the event the originals are destroyed by fire, flood, or other disasters.

Many companies fail to have a permanent crisis center in place. Pepsi-Cola Global set up an ad hoc crisis center in June 1993 after someone claimed to have found a syringe in a Diet Pepsi can. Within the next forty-eight hours, the company was bombarded by reports of syringes in cans from around the country.

Craig Weatherup, the chief executive, knew that the problem was not quality control. But he also knew that the company's trademark was at risk and he had to protect it.

Setting up a crisis center in a conference room, he spent most of the next seventy-two hours there. That small room allowed teamwork that would have been difficult had the major players been in different locations. When the company began to receive hundreds of calls from the media, customers, and franchisees, the conference-room team answered and returned up to three hundred phone calls a day. Members of the crisis team were surely inundated with "quips and sentences . . . paper bullets of the brain" which drained them of their "humors," as Benedick comments in *Much Ado About Nothing*. Nonetheless, they took this in stride.

Working together, they also updated fact sheets as often as ten times a day. Soon they obtained a video of their automated manufacturing lines showing that cans were turned upside down before they were filled and sealed. This demonstrated that *if* a syringe were ever in a can at the bottling plant, it would fall out before the can was sealed.

The tape was forwarded to TV stations, which broadcast it worldwide. This move, sending the message that Pepsi had nothing to hide and was already taking active measures to ensure the highest quality for its product, soon defused the crisis.

Meanwhile, the manager of a store in Denver forwarded to Pepsi a surveillance tape that showed a woman putting a syringe in an open Diet Pepsi can. In a final crisis control measure, Pepsi forwarded that tape, too, to every news station that wanted it. When the second video was broadcast, the crisis was officially over, as media organizations declared the scare a hoax.

LESSON SIX

"Make use change the stamp of nature."

—Hamlet

Crisis action plans should be tested and practiced regularly so that the crisis team has the routine down and is confident its approaches will work. Claudius has his crisis communication system in place, which gathers the critical information that Laertes is coming back from France "in secret."

Making the action plan known in advance to all who must play a role in its implementation is just as important. After all, the best-laid plans are worthless if no one knows they exist or how to use them.

Romeo and Juliet, for example, are famous victims of a communication system breakdown. Friar Laurence contrives a plausible plan for the star-struck lovers that entails Juliet drinking a potion that will render her lifeless but not dead. Her relatives, thinking she has died, will take her to the Capulet burial chamber and leave her. When she awakens, she'll meet Romeo and they'll run off to live happily ever after.

Unfortunately Friar Laurence relies on Friar John to inform Romeo of the plan. Friar John, however, is detained and doesn't reach Romeo in time. Romeo, in turn, thinking that Juliet has died, kills himself. When she awakens to find him dead, she kills herself. So much for secure communication systems.

Today corporate leaders should capitalize on the communication power of the Web. Putting up a crisis Web site—or adding a new section to an existing corporate Web site—is an efficient way to get critical information out to consumers, suppliers, employees, investors, and others in the corporate community. "All with one consent praise new-born gawds" or gadgets, as Ulysses says in

Troilus and Cressida, "though they are made and moulded of things past."

Pre-Web communication tools, such as press releases, faxes, and e-mails, should be sent to the press to let it know the information has been posted. In the case of product-related crises, Jim Horton, of Robert Marston & Associates, believes that an ideal Web site should include a message from the company president containing information on how consumers can remedy any problems caused by the crisis, whether it is a product recall or a natural disaster. If the company can't address certain concerns directly, it should put up links to Web sites that offer further technical expertise.

Companies should have an "open news area" where anyone can view information on the crisis, and a "closed news area" that includes expanded background information for the media. The closed news area can be made accessible only to those who have certain passcodes established in advance or immediately after the crisis hits.

To make sure that a breakdown in communication wouldn't happen to them, the Detroit Newspaper Agency anticipated a future crisis, put the appropriate systems in place, then communicated and practiced them. Consequently the agency was able to publish every day during the 1995 strike of the *Detroit News* and *Detroit Free Press.*

When labor talks grew difficult in 1992, chief executive Frank Vega and his team attended to details, including creating an emergency password system for the computers and installing locks that could be changed at a moment's notice. They also determined how many people they would need in the pressroom, composing room, and newsroom, so they could arrange to bring them in from other Gannett and Knight-Ridder newspapers. They figured out in advance where the temporary employees would park and how they would get to the building in the event of picketing.

When the inevitable crisis hit, twenty-five hundred employees walked out. Yet the presses continued to roll, and the company continued to function. Although both papers survived the strike, circulation remains down. Nonetheless, both papers are being published and the management has patience. "How poor are they that have not patience," Iago says in *Othello*. "What wound did ever heal but by degrees?"

LESSON SEVEN

"Tempt him with speed aboard; delay it not."

—Claudius, in *Hamlet*

Crises won't wait until everything's neatly sorted out. Speed is the essence of crisis management.

This point is made famously in Hamlet's "To be or not to be" soliloquy: "Thus conscience does make cowards of us all." Too much deliberation, precisely the type Hamlet himself indulges in, causes "enterprises of great pith and moment" to "lose the name of action."

Once Claudius sees that a crisis is at hand, he moves swiftly. As Master Ford says in *Merry Wives of Windsor,* "Better three hours too soon than a minute too late." With the pace of business accelerating daily, that line should be a mantra for high-level executives.

It certainly was for Dominique Raccah when she opened her publishing company, Sourcebooks Inc., from her home in 1987. One day she came home to find a note from the city of Naperville, Illinois, on her door. It told her she had to move the business elsewhere since local zoning didn't permit her to have three employees working from her house. The timing couldn't have been worse. Raccah's father was in the hospital, dying. She'd just come back from visiting him when she received the notice. Despite her personal pain, Raccah knew that if she delayed, she would lose her business.

Within days, she struck a deal to move her company to a Victorian house that a friend had converted to offices. He allowed her to hold off on paying the rent for the first two months. Since then, Raccah has acquired several other small publishers, and the formerly small, home-based business brings in about $10 million per year.

Dawdling can mean big losses for big businesses, like Motorola. The huge electronics corporation was the market leader when it began selling cellular phones in 1983. Unfortunately it delayed switching from its very profitable analog phones to digital models, which are expected to take over most of the market within two years. Although Motorola showed 25 percent annual sales growth in the mid-nineties, profits dropped sharply by 1996 as digital rivals such as Ericsson and Nokia continued gaining ground in the cellular phone industry.

Hoping to stage a comeback, Motorola bought 18 percent of Iridium, a global satellite communications system. However, Iridium hasn't been able to reach its target number of subscribers or revenue goals. Following the recent resignations of its two top executives, Iridium is now in the midst of debt restructuring.

LESSON EIGHT:

"Go but apart. Make choice of whom
your wisest friends shall hear and judge."

—Claudius, in *Hamlet*

Every crisis-management team should include at least one outside expert or wise counselor. Company insiders may be too close to a crisis to offer objective solutions; that's why Claudius specifically seeks outside counsel and advises Laertes to do the same. Moreover, asking only people close to the problem about the problem runs the risk that they may be the problem.

There's another reason to bring in outside counsel. Employees are often afraid to be direct with managers who "kill the messenger." Consider how Cleopatra responds when a messenger tells her that Antony has married Octavia back in Rome. She beats the messenger and warns him, "Though it be honest, it is never good to bring bad news."

In order to avoid the type of slanted information Cleopatra-types solicit, bringing in outsiders can help the crisis-management team sort out, analyze, and then act. While it can be costly and time-consuming to hire independent experts, the world-famous oil-well fire fighter Red Adair had it right when telling clients who objected to his fees that "If you think an expert is expensive, try hiring an amateur."

The Mondavi Winery dynasty learned the importance of outside experts when faced with a succession planning issue. When Robert Mondavi decided to hand over the reins of the family winery to his sons Michael, fifty-five, and Tim, forty-seven, they didn't anticipate the challenges that would arise.

Ultimately the Mondavis turned to Family Business Solutions, which specializes in succession in family businesses. Under the team's direction, the father and sons spent three weekend retreats together during which they engaged in activities such as writing down their life's goals. "That helped each of us define what we really wanted out of life," Michael says. The overall perspective of the outside advisors helped resolve the issues affecting the business.

Today the company is thriving. In spite of a grape-supply shortage caused by harvest problems in 1995 and 1996, Mondavi's net revenue has grown by more than 50 percent in the past three years, reaching $325 million in the fiscal year that ended in June 1998. Currently the stock trades at about $38 a share, and the company's wines are sold in eighty countries.

LESSON NINE

"There has been much throwing
about of brains."

—Rosencrantz, in *Hamlet*

When a crisis breaks, it's important not to be distracted from the task of keeping the company's core business moving forward as usual, lest it lose critical momentum that cannot be regained.

To continue running day-to-day operations as best they can during a crisis, executives should construct a "fire wall" between the crisis-management team and the business-operating team. Those who need not manage the crisis are thereby freed up to keep the everyday business functioning as smoothly as possible. The crisis team, independent of operating personnel, can then concentrate on confronting its immediate problem.

Often, however, creative new methods have to be employed to keep business moving as usual. Paul Lewis, chief executive of MC2 Corp., a technology company, learned that a large chunk of the company's building had collapsed in a blizzard in 1996. MC2, which supports the computer systems of seven hundred clients, including AT&T and Johnson & Johnson, found itself unable to operate. Making matters worse, MC2 executives found that they had misunderstood the business continuation on the insurance contract that they had purchased and relied on to bail out the company in just such a crisis. Lacking sufficient financial reserves, the company had to move its remaining equipment and thirty employees to its twelve-hundred-square-foot warehouse and operate there under extremely cramped conditions. Forced to rent desks and equipment to replace items that had been damaged, the company began falling behind on its bills. The IRS threatened to close it down for failing to meet its payroll taxes.

Rather than try to hide or gloss over what was going on in the crisis, MC2 took the opposite tack and began spreading the word of its problems. "They say best men are moulded out of faults," Mariana muses in *Measure for Measure,* "and, for the most, become much more the better for being a little bad."

Mariana's approach was tried in the company. The results of this risky, unconventional tactic were stunning. One client agreed to lend the firm the computers it needed to stay in business. The IRS, compared more often to Lady Macbeth than renowned for what she calls "the milk of human kindness," reevaluated the facts and reduced the interest the company owed on its payroll taxes. And MC2 Corp.'s bank raised its credit line from $50,000 to $200,000.

In April 1999 Volt Information Sciences, a publicly traded company, bought out MC2, which was projecting $5.5 million in revenue for that year. Volt aids Fortune 100 companies in meeting their telecommunications and information needs, and helps them with staffing and electronic publication and typsetting systems. In recognition of the value of Lewis's leadership, Volt is keeping him on as a division vice president at MC2.

LESSON TEN

"To thine own self be true."

—Polonius, in *Hamlet*

Especially in a crisis, top executives must feel that the company's position is the right and honorable one. "If your mind dislike anything," Horatio tells Hamlet, "obey it." Likewise, during the zenith of the crisis, corporate leaders should stop for a calm and dispassionate evaluation, *in human terms,* of the core issues involved, and side with integrity every time. "Speak what we feel," Albany says at the close of *King Lear,* "not what we ought to say."

Deciding whether the action prescribed will help build a "spotless reputation" for the company is critical in that process. When everything seems to be crashing down around them, executives then have the corporate core values, developed before the crisis ever broke, to fall back on.

Character in an organization, as in a person, develops when executives act in a habitually honorable way. The CEO and top team should strive daily to assure that their company is one where "nothing ill can dwell in such a temple," as Miranda says in *The Tempest.*

Observing this, the public usually grants its trust. Martin Marietta discovered this years ago upon the failure of two spacecraft built by another company which it had purchased a few months before. Martin Marietta took full responsibility and voluntarily returned to its customer the $22 million in profit it had received for the project.

To its amazement, accolades flowed in from the public, the media, and especially the customer. By doing what was right, Martin Marietta echoed the sentiments of Portia in *The Merchant of Venice:* "How far that little candle throws his beams! So shines a good deed in a naughty world."

General Motors offers a good example, too. For a long time, the company's image was slipping as rapidly as its share of the North American auto market—which fell from about 44 percent in 1980 to around 30 percent today. Although GM raked in $161 billion in 1998, it produced cars that weren't earning rave reviews for quality. There were plenty of reasons.

Because the company was so big, it has been struggling to overcome the inefficiencies that crop up in huge bureaucracies. Also, in 1998, it suffered strikes at two major plants in Flint, Michigan.

One hero in the situation turned out to be G. Richard Wagoner, Jr., a former North American operations chief who was named president in October 1998. Wagoner took the direct approach by cutting a thousand jobs. He, too, like Richard II's executive gardener, those "superfluous branches" did "lop away, that bearing boughs may live." This alone saved the company a much-needed $300 million.

Wagoner also improved automotive production and showed the kind of respect for automotive workers that Corin exemplifies in *As You Like It*: "Sir, I am a true labourer. I earn that I eat, get that I wear, owe no man hate, envy no man's happiness; glad of other men's good," he states with humility.

As a result of the improvements Wagoner has made, analysts are becoming excited about the company again. Wagoner and his colleagues helped to rebuild the company's reputation with honesty about what was wrong, thereby inspiring trust. "He's willing to face up to GM's problems in the marketplace, and that has made analysts comfortable and excited about the company," Greg L. Salchow of Roney Capital Markets told *Individual Investor* magazine.

Frank Portillo also shows how a leader's character can make all of the difference in a company's success. When the founder of Brown's Chicken and Pasta was roused from his sleep by an employee on January 9, 1993, he faced the shock of his life. A couple who franchised one of his restaurants, along with five of their employees, had been shot to death the night before. Their bodies had been left in the freezer and walk-in cooler.

As Portillo attended the series of funerals for his deceased employees, he was determined to provide leadership, despite the extreme pressure he was under. In the meantime, the father of a teenager who was killed sued Brown's for not having enough security at the store. "I still close my eyes and see it like a movie screen," Portillo says. "It was probably the most difficult time of my life."

Pictures of the restaurant in Palatine, Illinois, were broadcast constantly on the news for weeks. "The sense of death is most in apprehension," Isabella tells her brother in *Measure for Measure*. Customers experienced such apprehension that they gradually stopped going to any of the restaurants in the chain.

By 1994, the Chicago-based chain had shrunk from its peak of 125 stores to 74. Portillo started falling behind on paying his bills. His bankers, accountant, and lawyers pressured him to file for Chapter 11, which would have wiped his financial slate clean. Unwilling to yield, he found an attorney who worked for free and soon thereafter Portillo secured a $2 million loan from a new banker. Gradually he began to rebuild the chain. In the meantime, Portillo channeled his rage at the still-unsolved crime by helping other companies avoid similar tragedies.

At first he began talking to small business groups about security issues. Later, hoping to get to the root cause of crimes like the one that changed his life, he launched a reading program designed to help students at a local school in a high crime area.

Today the chain is still making a comeback under Portillo's brave leadership. "I don't know of any company that's been through what we've been through that has turned things around as well as we have," says Portillo. "We've got a lot of tenacity." Besides setting an inspiring example for his workers, Portillo has worked to stem crime in his community.

Basic values can help mightily during a crisis and turn a tragedy into a triumph. This fundamental message comes, in typical Shakespearean fashion, from *Richard II's* Mowbray, who has lived less than an honorable life. Finally realizing his loss, he elaborates the most profound lesson:

> Mine honor is my life, both grow in one.
> Take honor from me, and my life is done.
> Then, dear my liege, mine honor let me try;
> In that I live, and for that, will I die.

EPILOGUE

THE BUSINESS OF LIFE

"**N**o epilogue, I pray you," Theseus advises in *A Midsummer Night's Dream*, "for your play needs no excuse." This is one piece of advice from Shakespeare we won't follow. Yet neither will we make any excuse.

Rather our epilogue focuses on business lessons drawn from Shakespeare that extend beyond the world of commerce to the greatest business in the world—the business of life. In what Timon of Athens calls "life's uncertain voyage," all of us are CEOs. As such, we're responsible for managing our own profits and losses.

Coriolanus acts "as if a man were author of himself." Indeed he is, and we are.

All our actions affect the bottom line of our lives, which goes beyond financial data. Making a life is very different from making a living.

How we manage the business of life shapes everything from our choice of life partner, and the decision about whether to bring new life into the world, to the legacy we leave behind—in essence, how and why we live.

Like each of us, Shakespeare's characters are offered many viable options, both professionally and personally. Success in one may, or may not, mean success in the other. King Richard II fails utterly in his career, as he violates the lessons presented in Act III here on getting the job done. Yet after his complete professional failure, he grows into a successful human being. In contrast, Octavius Caesar is a winner at work but a hollow human being during off hours.

The correlation between professional success and personal happiness is low in Shakespeare. Among Shakespeare's most miserable characters are his kings. "Uneasy lies the head that wears a crown," King Henry IV says to end one of his depressing soliloquies on kingship. Indeed, many of Shakespeare's kings spend a fair amount of their time in office soliloquizing on their own misery.

What factors do make up the bottom line in life?

On this, Macbeth offers us clear guidance. Squandering impressive talents, Macbeth destroys everything in his path through his ambition for power. He realizes too late that the essential quality of his life has slipped away forever. "My way of life is fallen into the sear," he says. "And that which should accompany old age, as honor, love, obedience, troops of friends, I must not look to have."

To achieve these prime goals of life, Shakespeare offers some clear lessons on managing its essential business.

LESSON ONE

Recognize and manage the assets
we already possess.

Just as a company has its distinct personality, character, and strengths, so are we all endowed with certain precious qualities. "What a piece of work is a man!" exclaims Hamlet. "How noble in reason! How infinite in faculties! In form and moving, how express and admirable! In action how like an angel! In apprehension how like a god!" We humans are "the beauty of the world! the paragon of animals!" That, at least, is our potential.

The greatest of Shakespearean characters—like Hamlet and Falstaff, Rosalind and Cleopatra—fully appreciate the great gifts we've been given. Others take those gifts for granted. The Friar in *Much Ado About Nothing* says, "What we have, we prize not to the worth whilst we enjoy it." Yet "being lacked and lost, why then we . . . find the virtue that possession would not show us whilst it was ours."

Great Shakespearean characters not only appreciate assets given them, but also actively manage those assets. In essence, they live life to the hilt. "O gentlemen, the time of life is short!" the ever-impatient

Hotspur bellows out in *Henry IV, Part I*. "To spend that shortness basely were too long."

Such characters infuse an exuberance for life into all those around them. While Iago, Richard III, and Macbeth drain others of life's energy, and of life itself, the likes of Falstaff and Cleopatra energize and enliven all those lucky enough to share life with them.

The five characters featured in this book are all activists. The two kings—Henry V and Claudius—could be expected to be so, even though many of Shakespeare's kings are tragically passive. So are many of the Roman noblemen in *Julius Caesar*. Yet neither Portia, barred from men's rights and professions, nor Petruchio, of unexceptional status, act like victims after their fathers have died. Instead, they prove to be exceptional activists. As such, they exemplify the second lesson.

LESSON TWO

Assume responsibility.

This entails setting goals in life and taking risks to achieve those goals. To have idle assets on the balance sheet, whether in business or life, is a sign of poor management.

The key characters throughout Shakespeare are "masters of their fates," as Cassius explains to Brutus, and realize that responsibility "is not in our stars but in ourselves." Though of low birth and a woman in the male-dominated society of *All's Well That Ends Well*, Helena nonetheless insists that "our remedies oft in ourselves do lie, which we ascribe to heaven. The fated sky gives us free scope." She proceeds to act with full scope in an open sky.

The protagonists in Shakespeare who shirk responsibility, like Richard II and Antony late in life, tend to suffer. "I wasted time, and now doth time waste me," Richard II laments in prison before he is killed. Similarly, characters who rely too heavily on others suffer too. "O, how wretched is that poor man that hangs on princes' favors," says Cardinal Wolsey in *Henry VIII*.

Shakespeare's activists invariably attract attention "since things in motion sooner catch the eye than what stirs not," as Ulysses says in *Troilus and Cressida*. They become leaders who "in speech, in gait, in diet, in affections of delight . . . humors of blood" shape "the mark and glass, copy and book, that fashion[s] others," as Hotspur's widow says of him. In any company or society, they set the standards and show "how things are done around here." That's what King Henry V does through his stellar leadership as analyzed in Act I.

LESSON THREE

Consider credibility the most
valuable corporate and personal
equity, yet most vulnerable to
rapid depreciation.

"Tell truth and shame the devil," Hotspur guides us, and Polonius guides his son Laertes: "This above all: To thine own self be true, and it must follow, as the night the day, thou canst not then be false to any man." Even Shakespeare's sleaziest characters learn, before their closing scenes, that "truth will come to light," as Launcelot says in *The Merchant of Venice*.

The Bard teaches the value of credibility in deeds and words again through the example of Hotspur. The young warrior doubts Glendower, who boasts before the big battle: "I can call spirits from the vasty deep." Hotspur quickly retorts: "Why, so can I, or so can any man. But will they come when you do call for them?"

LESSON FOUR

Use mergers to compound strengths.
Yet realize that, to pay dividends, the bonds
between the partners must be both
strong and flexible.

As demonstrated in Act II, Petruchio turns a business proposition, "to wive it wealthily," into a fairly hostile takeover, and then into a hugely profitable merger in the business of his life. Though tamed, Katherine retains her falconlike temperament. She and Petruchio are among the strongest of Shakespearean characters, yet each learns the benefit of being flexible when dealing with the other.

Through these qualities they develop synergy, as is essential in any successful merger. Shakespeare conveys the beauty of a personal merger through the words, appropriately enough, of a common citizen in *King John*, who describes a colleague as "the half part of a blessed man, left to be finished by such as she," while she is "a fair divided excellence, whose fullness of perfection lies in him." Together, "two such silver currents, when they join, do glorify the banks that bound them in" as their "two such . . . streams [are] made one."

LESSON FIVE

Consider personnel selection to be
as critical in choosing friends in life
as it is in finding bosses, colleagues,
and subordinates in business.

"Words are easy, like the wind; faithful friends are hard to find," Shakespeare writes. But once found and their worth proven, or, as Polonius instructs Laertes, "their adoption tried, grapple them unto thy soul with hoops of steel." Deep friendship furnishes one of life's greatest treasures, even to that hard and unpoetic Bolingbroke: "I count myself in nothing else so happy as in a soul remembering my good friends."

LESSON SIX

Appreciate how human frailties
and failings should inspire tolerance
and a desire to help associates
realize their full potential.

This requires a measured temperament, especially in executives and others with authority. They should possess tolerance for inherent human flaws but intolerance for human indifference, negligence, and laziness.

No Shakespearean hero is ideal, and each of his villains has some admirable attributes. Every character displays some fine traits and many flaws. The Bard put the point most poetically in Sonnet 35 when writing that just as "roses have thorns, and silver fountains mud . . . and loathsome canker lives in sweetest bud, [so] all men make faults." Claudius and Bolingbroke have a competence that Falstaff and Bottom clearly lack. Yet Falstaff and Bottom possess imagination, openness, and life force that these executive types lack.

All of us, but especially those in positions of trust and power, should exercise restraint. "O, it is excellent to have a giant's strength!" another of Shakespeare's strong and intelligent women, Isabella, tells us in *Measure for Measure,* "but it is tyrannous to use it like a giant." Executives with "a giant's strength" must be particularly sensitive to others' feelings and avoid proceeding as Sebastian in *The Tempest* accuses Gonzalo of proceeding: "The truth you speak doth lack some gentleness and time to speak it in. You rub the sore, when you should bring the plaster."

Whether in corporate business or in the business of life, tolerance includes being able to disagree without being disagreeable, much as Tranio instructs in *The Merchant of Venice:* "Do as adversaries do in law— strive mightily but eat and drink as friends."

LESSON SEVEN

Brace for a crisis and recover
as quickly as possible.

No business or life can be fully insured against occasional disasters. Life's challenges must be met head-on, given that life goes on. As Petruchio shows us in Act II, this may require a reconfiguring of priorities and even of behavior.

Unmatched by anything in business, a personal crisis can overwhelm a life and seem interminable. "Grief makes one hour ten," Bolingbroke says in *Richard II*. But it can be partly alleviated by sharing. "Give sorrow words," Malcolm urges Macduff, after informing him that Macbeth has slaughtered his wife and children, "The grief that does not speak, whispers [to] the overfraught heart and bids it break."

During a crisis, recognizing the bountiful assets we have and how "the fated sky gives us free scope" speeds the realization that "the world may laugh again," as Gloucester says in *Henry VI, Part II*.

LESSON EIGHT

Practice fiscal responsibility.

Since life is not an annuity, fiscal responsibility is as integral to an individual's and family's bottom line as to a corporation's. In all cases, financial leverage used temperately can fuel prosperity. But used excessively by those "whose large style agrees not with the leanness of his purse," as Gloucester says in *Henry VI, Part II*, it can lead to ruin.

LESSON NINE

Prize reputation as *the* core
competency in the accounting
of corporate and personal life.

"Good name in man and woman," Iago tells Othello, "is the immediate jewel of their souls. Who steals my purse, steals trash . . . but he that filches from me my good name . . . makes me poor indeed."

Having a "spotless reputation" is "the purest treasure mortal times afford," as Mowbray says in *Richard II*. And losing it is the one business transaction where turnarounds are nonexistent. "Reputation, reputation, reputation! O, I have lost my reputation! I have lost the immortal part of myself, and what remains is bestial," Cassio says in *Othello*.

These nine lessons can help any executive move beyond considering a standard of living and start to appraise standards for life. They can contribute immeasurably to that bottom line of everything "that . . . should accompany old age, as honor, love, obedience, troops of friends."

Beyond doing well, it means doing good. It means having "a good heart," as Henry V says after his staggering professional successes. "A good heart, Kate, is the sun and the moon—or, rather, the sun, and not the moon—for it shines bright and never changes, but keeps its course truly."